• **Bartholom**

WALK EDINBURGH
& THE PENTLANDS
by Richard Hallewell
Illustrations by Rebecca Johnstone

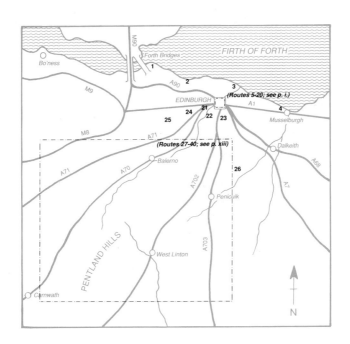

Bartholomew
A Division of HarperCollins*Publishers*

British Library Cataloguing in Publication Data

Hallewell, Richard
      Walk Edinburgh & the Pentlands.
      1. Edinburgh - Visitors' guides 2. Scotland.
      Pentland Hills - Visitors' guides
      I. Title
      914.13404859

      ISBN 0-7028-1280-3

Published by Bartholomew, a Division of HarperCollins*Publishers*.
12 Duncan Street, Edinburgh EH9 1TA.

First published 1991
© Bartholomew 1991

Printed in Great Britain by Bartholomew,
HarperCollins*Manufacturing*, Edinburgh.

ISBN 0-7028-1280-3

Assistance has been provided in the production of this guide by
the Scottish Rights of Way Society, the Pentland Ranger
Service and the Edinburgh Tourist Board.

About this book

This is a selection of walks through the city of Edinburgh, its environs and the Pentland Hills, each of which can be completed within a day. The city routes cover the finest streets and parks in Edinburgh, while other low-lying routes visit nearby towns and beauty spots. The Pentland routes include all Rights of Way and accepted footpaths through the hills.

Each route is graded according to its level of difficulty, and wherever specialist hill-walking equipment is required this is specified on the contents page. There is a description of each route, including information on the character and condition of the paths for the country walks, and a brief description of the major points of interest along the way, plus a detailed sketch map of the route to aid navigation. This guide supplies all the necessary information to complete each walk, but additional useful information for the city walks can be found in the Edinburgh Street Guide, while the Bartholomew Pentland Hills Walking Map is recommended for the hill routes

Car parks, where available, are indicated on the route maps and on the two sub-area maps covering the centre of Edinburgh and the Pentlands (p. i and p. xiv respectively). The availability of public conveniences and public transport on particular routes is listed on the contents page and at the start of each walk. The location of all the routes is shown on the main area map, at the front of the book, and/or on the sub-area maps of Edinburgh and the Pentlands.

The following introduction provides a summary of the geography, history, literature and wildlife of the area. There is also a section of Advice to Walkers in the Pentlands section, which should be read before setting out on the hill routes. The Pentlands offer no great dangers, but it never pays to become lax in taking safety precautions.

I hope you will find this an interesting selection of walks. Additional local routes can be found in one of the companion volumes in this series: Walk Lothian, the Borders and Fife.

Key

●●●	Route	◁28 --	Other Routes in Book	**1 foot = 0.3m**
===	Metalled Road	〰〰	Marshland	**1 mile = 1.6km**
++++	Railway	▲▲	Coniferous Woodland	
Ⓟ	Parking	♦♦	Broad-leaved Woodland	
(50m)	Contour: shaded area is above height indicated	i	Information Centre	

INTRODUCTION

Edinburgh: Description and History

(Figures in italics refer to individual walks)

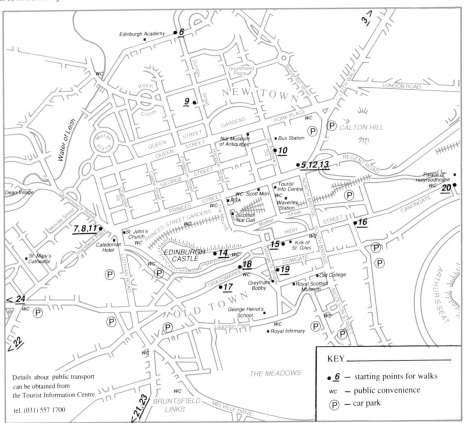

KEY _____

• **6** — starting points for walks

wc — public convenience

(P) — car park

Details about public transport
can be obtained from
the Tourist Information Centre.

tel. (031) 557 1700

Edinburgh is Scotland's capital and its most historic city. It is also, arguably, the most picturesque city in Britain, with a great density of fine architecture, monuments and parks within a small area. This compactness makes the city ideal for exploration on foot, and the city walks in this guide *(5-21)* pass through all the areas of greatest interest in Edinburgh's historic centre. The map above shows this central section, and indicates the starting points of the city walks.

As can be seen from the map, the centre of Edinburgh can be divided into two distinct sections: the Old Town and the New Town. The Old Town straddles the low, steep ridge between Holyroodhouse and the castle. Its streets are narrow and its buildings tall – up to eleven storeys where the City Chambers drops down into Cockburn St *(15)* – and built in a bewildering variety of styles. In places, a symmetrical, neo-Classical facade will be seen, but such rarities serve only to emphasise the essentially haphazard nature of the development of the ridge, where no sign of planning can be seen in the layout of the streets or the design of the buildings. Tenements (or 'lands', to use the Edinburgh word) were squeezed into the gaps left by the destruction of their predecessors, and cantilevered out across the road, or over the entrance to some narrow close, or 'wynd', to make the best use of the space in this painfully narrow strip of development. Brass plates along the walls of the High St *(15)* mark the positions of old closes, their entrances long since buried under new structures.

The architecture of the Old Town is principally Scots vernacular, plus the imitations and interpretations of the 19th and 20th centuries, and the skyline is full of corner turrets and crow-stepped gables.

The New Town is (as it was meant to be) a complete contrast. The streets are not narrow and crooked, but broad and straight; the buildings are low, wide and well lit, not tall, narrow and small-windowed; and the anarchism of development and design is replaced by an austere and rigorous Classicism.

These two towns within a single city are a Jekyll and Hyde pair; apparently opposite, yet each incomplete without the other. The finest view from the Old Town is north, across the grid-iron streets of the New; the finest view from the New Town is south, across Princes Street Gardens *(14,17)* to the cluttered ridge of the Old, and the sprawling castle *(14)* on its massive, bare rock.

The buildings are like visual memoranda of Scottish history, much of which took place against the theatrical backdrop which they provide. Scarcely a notable personage, army or movement failed to pass through Edinburgh's streets, and many of the nation's famous characters remain here yet, lying in the old graveyards around the city centre. David Hume and William Playfair are in the Calton Cemetery *(13)*; Adam Smith in the Canongate *(16)*, with David Rizzio (Mary Queen of Scots' murdered courtier), the mad poet Robert Fergusson, and Burns' 'Clarinda'. James Craig, the original designer of the New Town, is buried in Greyfriars *(18)* with the poets Allan Ramsay and Duncan Ban MacIntyre. Greyfriars Bobby is also there – the faithful Skye terrier who lived by his dead master's grave for fourteen years; while the old enemies of the Covenanting wars, James Graham, Marquis of Montrose, and Archibald Campbell, Marquis of Argyll, reassembled after their grisly executions at the Mercat Cross, lie on opposite sides of the Kirk of St. Giles *(15)*, and John Knox is lost somewhere beneath the cobbles and tarmac of Parliament Sq *(15)*.

What attracted these people to Edinburgh was its position as Scotland's capital: the seat of the nation's monarch and parliament. That the city achieved this prominence was due largely to the defensive properties of Castle Rock.

There are seven hills in Edinburgh – Arthur's Seat *(20)*, Calton *(13)*, Corstorphine *(24)*, Craiglockhart, Braid *(23)*, Blackford and Castle Rock *(15,17)* – of which the last is, though not the highest, certainly the most dramatic. It is the basalt core of an extinct volcano. Through the centuries, the softer rocks were eroded, leaving a low hill: virtually sheer on three sides, and approached along a narrow ridge on the fourth. The site had obvious defensive potential, and would seem to have been colonised by the various tribes who inhabited the area before and after the Roman period. Amongst these tribes were the Northumbrians, whose early 7th-century king, Edwin, is generally thought to have given his name to the fort on the rock – Edwin's Burgh (Edwin's Castle) – although there are other theories about the origin of the name, and it may come from a Gaelic root.

The earliest buildings must have been on the crown of the rock, but nothing remains from this early period. The oldest building in Edinburgh, however, is within the castle walls: St Margaret's Chapel, built around 1090 for Queen Margaret, the influential English wife of King Malcolm Canmore.

Prior to Margaret's time, Edinburgh had simply been one of a number of residences of the peripatetic Scottish court. Subsequently, an increasingly anglicised court made more use of this southern stronghold until, by the time of James II (the mid 15th century) it was *de facto* capital.

The castle which has gradually developed around the chapel is not so much a single entity as an assortment of buildings; built by various monarchs when the need arose and the exchequer allowed. The finest buildings are the Great Hall, built by James IV in the early 16th century, and the small palace looking over the castle entrance, where James VI was born in 1566.

On the ridge leading up to the west of the castle, a settlement began to emerge; slowly spreading eastwards. In 1128, David I founded the Abbey of Holyroodhouse *(16,20)*, under the lee of the grassy mound of Arthur's Seat, in thanks (or so legend has it) for a narrow escape from an accident whilst hunting a stag in the hills nearby. The establishment of the abbey effectively defined the shape of the Old Town as it remains to this day. The connecting road between the castle and the abbey followed the line of the present Royal Mile – Castlehill, Lawnmarket *(both 14)*, High St *(15)*, Canongate *(16)* – while the buildings which the Augustinian canons of the abbey were permitted to build by the roadside grew into the separate burgh of Canongate.

The Palace of Holyroodhouse originated as the guest house for the abbey. The site was more comfortable than the exposed castle, and successive monarchs began to spend more time there, until, at the start of the 16th century, James IV decided to formalise the arrangement by building a Royal Palace. All that remains of his building is the north-west tower, now echoed by a symmetrical copy at the other end of the facade: designed, as was the rest of the current building, by Sir William Bruce in the late 17th century. This new building was constructed for Charles II.

The earliest settlements around the castle were undefended, and the residents often paid a high price for their proximity to one of the principal royal strongholds in Scotland. During the 13th, 14th and 15th centuries, as a succession of English kings attempted to annexe Scotland, the castle became a vital piece in the game of war, and successive armies, English and Scottish, would descend upon the town for siege or assault.

Perhaps the most famous assault of the castle was that by Thomas Randolph, who captured it from the English for Robert the Bruce in 1314, on the eve of the Scottish victory at Bannockburn; creeping up the Castle Rock with a small body of men and opening the gates from the inside. There were many attempts however, and as late as 1745 the Jacobite army billeted in the Old Town was dodging cannonballs fired by the Hanoverian garrison from the Half-Moon battery, behind the entrance gate. The firing is reported to have caused more casualties amongst the people of Edinburgh than in the Highland army.

Attempts were made to protect the settlement from these invasions. As early as 1450 a wall was built around a small area beneath the castle, and this area was enlarged when a new wall was started in 1513. This was the Flodden Wall, planned in a fit of panic in anticipation of an English invasion, following the disastrous defeat of the Scottish army at Flodden, and the death of James IV and around 10,000 men. The panic passed and the work dragged, but the wall was finally completed, and no major development was attempted beyond it until the 18th century; a restriction which was to have a profound effect on the development of Edinburgh.

The line of this wall can be followed through the city streets. It started at the south-eastern corner of the castle and dropped down to the western end of the Grassmarket *(17,18)* (where the West Port, or gate, was situated), continued up the Vennel (a section is still visible here) and Heriot Pl then cut east, along Lauriston Pl *(all 18)*. Beyond this it continued along Teviot Pl, Bristo Pl, Bristo Port, South College St and Drummond St, before turning north along the Pleasance and St. Mary's St *(15,16)*, leading up to the eastern end of the North Loch, which provided protection for the city to the north. This loch originally filled the area now covered by Princes Street Gardens. Given the large population which lived by it, and the sanitary standards of the time, it must have been a particularly noisome stretch of water. This situation cannot have been improved by the fact that the shambles, or flesh-market, was located by the waterside until the 18th century.

It can be seen that Edinburgh effectively became a medieval, walled city just at the time when the medieval period was finishing elsewhere in Europe. The concentration on development within the Flodden Wall continued up to the dawn of the Enlightenment, by which time there was a population of almost forty thousand housed within an area of less than 140 acres (57ha).

Maps of the Old Town from the 18th century and earlier show it to have had, in isolation, a shape not unlike that of the skeleton of a fish; with the castle at the head and Holyroodhouse at the tail; the road between them forming the spine and the wynds and closes (many more then than now) to north and south the smaller bones. These alleyways were longest in the city itself, and shorter along the Canongate, outside the city walls.

Canongate *(16)* was the preferred residence of the Scottish nobility, where they could build large mansions, a little apart from the crowds of Edinburgh. Following the Union of the Crowns (1603) and of the Parliaments (1707), and the effective removal of power from Edinburgh, there was little reason for the nobility to keep a town house in Scotland, and the area fell into general disrepair. It was not until the 20th century that the Canongate was tidied up, and some of the remaining mansions – notably Moray House and Huntly House *(both 16)* – were returned to their original splendour.

Such nobles as chose to live within the city walls, in the 16th and 17th century, built their mansions along the Cowgate *(15,18)*, on the southern edge of the city. It is hard now to believe that this sunken, gloomy street, with its crumbling tenements, was once the most fashionable avenue in Edinburgh.

For the rest of the inhabitants of the city, privacy and comfort were at a minimum. The descriptions of foreign visitors invariably strike a note of horrified admiration. The High Street was impressive, and the lands – built up to 14 storeys by the 18th century – quite unique, but the stench was appalling, with effluent in piles in the closes, or running along the steep guttering (it was emptied from the windows of the lands at a set time each day, accompanied by the warning cry of 'gardyloo!'). Genteel visitors were shocked by the familiarity between the different classes, though such distinctions were inevitably blurred when rich merchants and lawyers and the uwashed poor lived up a common stair: the rich on the upper floors, the poor on the lower.

All agreed it was a lively town though. Before the Union of the Crowns it was the home of the Scottish court, and remained the seat of Parliament for a century after that. Whenever Parliament was in session, the Riding of Parliament would take place – when the Crown Jewels were escorted up the High St to Parliament Hall *(15)* – and the town would be filled with Highland and Lowland noblemen and their followers. There were weekly markets in the Grassmarket, executions at the Mercat Cross and the Grassmarket, and occasional riots by the unruly Edinburgh Mob.

The Mob was, effectively, the political voice of the commoners. During the discussions over the Act of Union, its strongly patriotic views were largely ignored, but it proved rather more effective in the famous Porteous Riot, some 30 years later.

The riot – described in Scott's *The Heart of Midlothian* – stemmed from the rash actions of Captain Porteous of the Town Guard, who ordered his men to fire on the restive crowd at a public execution – an act for which he was subsequently imprisoned in the Tolbooth (the old Edinburgh jail; situated opposite the entrance to St. Giles' and demolished in 1817). Upon learning that, somewhat tactlessly, the government intended to pardon Porteous, the Mob sprung him from the Tolbooth and lynched him. This was one of the rare occasions when a riot led to violence, but it exemplifies the ordered single-mindedness with which the Mob – orchestrated by various individuals – operated; pursuing popular justice with a detached self-righteousness. When a rope was taken from a shop in the West Bow (now the Olde Curiosity Shoppe) *(18)* for the hanging, a guinea was left in its place.

Against the backdrop of the Old Town, the great events of Scotland's last two centuries of independence took place. Most of these were manifestations of the religious squabbles which were endemic throughout Europe at the time: the Reformation, with John Knox preaching in St Giles' *(15)* against the Catholic Mary Queen of Scots; the signing of the National Covenant in Greyfriars churchyard in 1638 (a bond, calling for the defence of Scottish Presbyteriansim against the Episcopalianism of Charles I: this document can be seen in the museum in Huntly House *(16)*), the subsequent Wars of the Covenant, and the execution of the Royalist general Montrose; the Restoration in 1660, further battles between Royalists and Covenanters, and the imprisonment (ironically, also in Greyfriars churchyard), execution or deportation of the defeated Covenanters. Finally, it was the scene of the signing of the Act of Union itself: passed by the

Scottish parliament on the 16th of January, 1707, under intense political, economic and military pressure from England, and to the fury of the vast majority of Scots. The passing of the Scottish Parliament was to have profound implications for Edinburgh.

The people of the city were employed almost entirely in service industries – from bootmakers, wig makers and clothiers down to the 'caddies': beggars who acted as messengers and guides – and the removal of power from the city, and thus of the rich and titled who pursued it, and the councillors and clerks who supported it, sent Edinburgh into decline. When the Lord Chancellor passed the Act of Union, he was heard to say 'there's the end of an auld sang', and it seemed that he might have spoken the epitaph for Edinburgh. In fact, the city was to recover its position, but not before the final refrain of another 'auld sang' was heard.

In 1745 Prince Charles Edward Stuart was in Edinburgh; giving balls in the Palace of Holyroodhouse and drumming up support for what proved to be the last Jacobite rebellion. He was on his way south, but by the start of 1746 he was heading north again, on his way to defeat at Culloden Moor and the end of any hope of a return of the Stuart dynasty to the throne of Great Britain.

The rebellion attracted supporters for a number of religious and social reasons, but part of its appeal was patriotic. The Union was still greatly resented, and the inept management of Scottish affairs led to frustration among the powerless nobility; even those who broadly supported the House of Hanover. After 1746, however, both the Hanovers and the Union were firmly entrenched, and the majority of the Scots nobility, now relieved of a tricky moral decision, knuckled down to make the most of it.

The prevailing mood was a mixture of humiliation and relief. Humiliation at the latter end of Scotland's long independence, and relief at the nation's first hope of real and prolonged peace and prosperity. This mood is perfectly caught in a document entitled *Proposals for carrying on certain Public Works in the City of Edinburgh*, which was published in 1752. This pamphlet contained the idea for the New Town: describing the crumbling decay of Edinburgh's buildings and the removal of the nobility to London; reviewing Scotland's past poverty and future potential and suggesting how Edinburgh might best improve itself to make the most of these opportunites, and entice the genteel back to Scotland.

The document was largely inspired by George Drummond, the Lord Provost of Edinburgh, and contained ideas which had been germinating in his mind for almost 30 years; ideas which were to prove highly attractive to a nation which, unknowingly, was approaching its Golden Age. By the second half of the 18th century, Voltaire could say, his irony laced with truth, 'Rules of taste in all the arts, from epic poems to gardening, come from Scotland'. The finest lasting monument to this period was the New Town of Edinburgh. Incredibly, within less than a century of the publication of the *Proposals* the plan outlined had been completed, and the anticipated results – prosperity, influence and gentility – had been realised.

The first tentative steps in the new development were taken in 1763, with the building of George Sq *(19)*, to the south of the Old Town. Then, in 1765, a contract was awarded to build the North Bridge, across the North Loch, and a year later a competition was held to find a plan for an extension of the city to the north.

James Craig was only 23 when he produced his winning plan: a symmetrical, grid-iron pattern of straight streets, squares and terraces, closely following the neo-Classical tastes of the period. The area which he planned covered Queen St, George St *(both 10)* and Princes St *(14,17)*, St. Andrew Sq and Charlotte Sq *(both 10)*, and the streets in between. The streets were named partly in flattery of the royal family, and partly as an allegory of the Union, with St. Andrew Sq being balanced by St. George's (though this name was subsequently changed, in deference to Queen Charlotte), and Rose St by Thistle St. Craig designed none of the houses: that was to be left to the individual architects.

The success of Edinburgh's New Town was assisted by the emergence of a stream of exceptional architects – Robert Adam, William

Playfair, William Chambers, Robert Reid, William Stark, Archibald Elliot and others – who were not only gifted, but were willing to subjugate their gifts to the creation of a unified whole. Sadly, more recent architects have proved unable to make the same sacrifices, and 20th-century infills tend to refer only ironically, if at all, to the austere canons of Classicism.

Neo-Classical buildings were built in the Old Town – notably the City Chambers *(15)*, the Old College of Edinburgh University *(18,19)* and the remodelled Parliament Sq *(15)* – but it was in the New Town that the style reached its apogee: a concerted whole, with large, single structures – such as Register House *(5,12,13)*, The National Gallery and the Royal Scottish Academy *(both 14)*, St Andrew's Church *(10)* and the Royal High School *(13)* – surrounded and linked by rows of splendid terraces. Nothing could be less like the hectic Old Town than the calm avenues of the New. Even today, though the centre of the city is busy with traffic, the more remote terraces retain the secluded tranquility which must have been their primary appeal to the prosperous middle-classes of 18th- and 19th-century Edinburgh.

The first building in the New Town was constructed in 1767, in Thistle Court *(10)*. Financial incentives were given to the builder, and to those who chose to follow him, and, initially, there was no pressure for architectural conformity. By 1791, however, the Town Council were asking Robert Adam to provide a unified plan for Charlotte Sq, and this was the approach which was subsequently followed.

The town was developed in blocks: the Northern New Town (between Heriot Row and Fettes Row) *(9,10)*; the Moray Estate (Moray Pl to Randolph Cres) *(9,10)*; the terraces around Calton Hill *(13)*; Sir Henry Raeburn's development to the west of the Water of Leith *(7)*, and, in the 1820s, the West End, around Melville St *(8,11)*.

In the meantime, the North Loch was drained and replaced by Princes Street Gardens, while a direct link was provided between the new housing and the shops of the Old Town by the construction of the Mound *(14)*: a sloping causeway, built of earth taken from the foundations of the growing New Town.

By the middle of the 19th century the finest crop of architects had gone, and the cult of neo-Classicism was over, yet the town continued to expand: fuelled by the Industrial Revolution (attracting country people to the towns) and a spiralling population. The Classical terraces gave way to Victorian tenements and areas of free-standing villas *(21)*. One by one, the city began to swallow up its neighbouring villages.

Broughton *(12)* and Greenside *(13)* had already disappeared beneath the eastern New Town, which now began to spread along Leith Walk *(5)* until the city was joined to its previously independent port of Leith *(3)*, and to the fishing villages of Newhaven and Granton to the west; eventually reaching as far as the little white-washed village of Cramond *(1,2)* at the mouth of the River Almond. To the East of Leith, along the waterfront, 20th-century development joined the city to the old resort town of Portobello, and stretched further to merge with the towns of Fisherrow, Musselburgh and Inveresk *(all 4)*, although these are still, technically, outside the city. To the west, the city incorporated Corstorphine *(24)*, at the foot of its wooded hill, and Dean Village *(7)*, a mill town near the West End, in the valley of the Water of Leith. To the south, it surrounded Morningside and the little mill village of Colinton *(22)*, though the building stopped short of the white-washed cottages of Swanston *(27)*, at the foot of the Pentlands.

One of the charms of Edinburgh is that these villages were left largely untouched by the surrounding development, and retain their own distinctive shape and charm. Similarly, a number of mansion houses and castles which were built in the countryside surrounding the capital were not demolished when the new housing reached them, and can still be seen. Examples include Gayfield House *(12)*, Merchiston Tower *(21)*, Hermitage of Braid *(23)* and Inverleith House *(6)*, in the Botanic Gardens. The gardens themselves are splendid, and there are miles of footpaths through the 70 acres (28ha) surrounding the house.

During the early part of the Industrial Revolution, the tiny river of the Water of Leith supported a large number of mills and small industrial villages – Dean Village, Colinton, Juniper Green, Currie *(both 30)*, Balerno *(31)* – but as industry became heavier and required greater sources of power, these early mills were abandoned, and Edinburgh – which lacked a major river – was passed over for industrial development in favour of Glasgow and the other towns in the Clyde valley; thus, though there are some legacies of the Industrial Age in Edinburgh and the surrounding area – notably the Union Canal of 1822 *(21,25)*, and the mining villages to the east of the Pentlands *(26)* – the city has avoided many of the problems associated with the decline of heavy industry.

Edinburgh: Literature

Just as Edinburgh has been blessed with more than its share of fine architects, so it has attracted and produced a large number of important literary figures. Before the Union of the Crowns, writers were attracted by the court, and the prospect of patronage, while during the period of the city's greatest glory (the end of the 18th and the start of the 19th century), they were drawn by its reputation, and by the presence of numerous publishing houses and established literary giants, such as Sir Walter Scott

Furthermore, just as Edinburgh's architecture can be divided into the vernacular and the Classical, so its writers have worked in two distinct schools: Scots and English. There has been a gradual swing from the former to the latter, but no clean chronologial break: as early as 1614, **Drummond of Hawthornden** – who lived at Hawthornden Castle, above Roslin Glen *(26)* – was writing in English, while Scots poetry continues to be written today, and has been used effectively in the 20th century by such major figures as **Sydney Goodsir Smith** and **Hugh MacDiarmid.**

The Golden Age for Scots poetry, however, was in the 15th and 16th centuries, when Scots was the language of the court and of educated men. The poetry of writers such as **Robert Henryson, William Dunbar** and **Gavin Douglas** was not a self-conscious reconstruction, but an entirely natural use of their native tongue.

William Dunbar left a brief glimpse of Edinburgh near the start of the 16th century in his poem *To the Merchantis of Edinburgh*: a complaint about the condition of the city's streets, and the clutter of 'krames' and 'luckenbooths' – the merchants' stalls which filled the High St, and which were even built up against the walls of St. Giles'. Despite Dunbar's censure, these were to remain a feature of the city until the 19th century.

> *May nane pas throw your principall gaittis*
> *for stink of haddockis and of scattis*
> *for cryis of carlingis and debaittis,*
> *for fensum flyttingis of defame.*
> *Think ye not schame,*
> *befoir strangeris of all estattis*
> *that sic dishonour hurt your name!*

carlingis: old women   *fensum:* offensive
flyttingis: arguments

During the 18th and early 19th centuries, the Scots-English literary debate was at its height. Following the Union of Parliaments, the Scots suffered something of an identity crisis, and writers had to decide whether this condition could best be alleviated by following the lead of Drummond or of Dunbar

Once the New Town had been established, its denizens quickly adopted English; taking lessons in pronunciation, and buying books which listed the Scotticisms most carefully to be avoided. Yet, paradoxically, they retained an interest in the mother tongue, and if they chose to see Edinburgh as the 'Athens of the North', they did not forget the 'Doric', though the adoption of this term ensured that Scots would, henceforth, be seen as a rustic, inferior language, spoken by the peasant inhabitants of an impossibly romantic pastoral idyll.

One of the first Edinburgh authors to profit from this growing sentimentality was **Allan Ramsay** (the father of the famous portrait painter).

Ramsay was a wig-maker, but his interest in literature led him to open a bookstall in the luckenbooths around St. Giles', and to open a short-lived theatre in Carrubber's Cl *(15)*, in 1736. He also published the *Tea Table Miscellany*, a collection of Scots songs, and a number of works of his own, the best known and most popular of which was *The Gentle Shepherd* (1725): a bucolic melodrama. Ramsay's various ventures proved successful, encouraging a generation of Scots poets, and purchasing for him a fine retirement house near the castle. This curious, octagonal building - nicknamed 'Goose Pie' – was subsequently incorporated into Ramsay Gdns *(14)*.

Amongst Ramsay's contemporaries, in the first flush of the Scottish Enlightenment, were **James Thomson**, who left Edinburgh University to publish *The Seasons* (1730) – one of the key early works of Romanticism – and **David Hume**, the great sceptical philosopher and author of the *Treatise of Human Nature* (1739-40). Hume was one of those who made the move from the Old Town to the New. At first he lived in Riddle's Ct, then he moved across the Lawnmarket to James Ct *(14)* – an area also inhabited by the young **James Boswell**, who was later to write the classic biography *The Life of Johnson* (1791) – before finally moving to St. David St (so-called in an ironic reference to the notorious atheism of its most famous resident), off St. Andrew Sq *(10)*.

Hume's controversial opinions encouraged a clutch of Scottish philosophers in the following years, the most important of whom was **Adam Smith** of Kirkcaldy; remembered now not for his moral philosophy, but for the *Inquiry into the Nature and Causes of the Wealth of Nations* (1776): one of the first and most influential books on economics. Smith kept a house in Panmure Cl *(16)*, just off the Canongate.

The elegant, Augustan English of Hume and Smith represents one side of Edinburgh's literary output, but writers were still emerging who were willing to follow Ramsay's lead. One of the finest was **Robert Fergusson**, who died in 1774, at the age of 24, in the Bedlam by Forrest Rd *(18,19)* (on the site now occupied by the Bedlam Theatre).

Fergusson is the ultimate Old Town poet; writing his verses in a rich, pungent vernacular, and using the life and the characters of the narrow closes and their numerous drinking howffs as his subject matter.

> *Now some to Porter, some to Punch,*
> *Some to their Wife, and some their Wench,*
> *Retire, while noisy Ten-hours Drum*
> *Gars a' your Trades gae dandering Hame.*
> *Now mony a Club, jocose and free,*
> *Gie a' to Merriment and Glee,*
> *Wi' sang and Glass, they fley the Pow'r*
> *O' Care that wad harrass the Hour...*
> (from *Auld Reekie*)
> *gars:* makes *dandering:* sauntering
> *Auld Reekie:* Edinburgh

Fergusson's output was small, but his work was to prove an inspiration to the most important Scots poet of them all: **Robert Burns**. When Fergusson died, he was buried in an unmarked grave in the Canongate churchyard *(16)*, but Burns subsequently provided a stone and an epitaph; albeit, rather inaptly, in stilted English:

> *No sculptur'd marble here, nor pompous lay,*
> *No story'd urn nor animated bust;*
> *This simple stone directs pale SCOTIA's way*
> *To pour her sorrows o'er her POET's dust.*

Burns was in Edinburgh to publish the 'Edinburgh Edition' (1787) of his poems, and the warm reception which the town accorded the poet – described by the writer **Henry Mackenzie** as a 'heaven-taught ploughman' – marked the death of Scots as a medium for anything other than bucolic sentimentality for a century and a half. There is a statue of Burns in Leith *(3)*, and he shares the museum at Lady Stair's House *(14)* with **Scott** and **Stevenson**.

During Burns' stay in Edinburgh, he had a famous meeting with the young **Walter Scott**, at Sciennes Hill House (to the south-east of the Meadows). Scott marks the start of the 'second generation' of the Scottish Enlightenment, and was largely responsible for spreading a knowledge of Scotland's history throughout Europe. His importance to the country is shown by the huge monument which was built to him in 1844, on

Princes St, the busiest street in the city *(14)*.

Scott was born in College Wynd, near the top of what is now Guthrie St *(18)*, and later lived in George Sq *(19)* and Castle St *(10)*. He developed an early interest in Scottish history and, marrying it to the contemporary taste for the Romantic, created a hugely successful sequence of historical poems and novels.

His interest in Romantic literature was stirred by his early reading of the works of **James Macpherson**: a Highlander, whose bogus 'translations' of Gaelic sagas had a great influence upon European literature at the end of the 18th century. Macpherson's work can be seen as the origin of the Celtic Twilight myth, and it was the misfortune of Scottish literature that Scott, for all his historical accuracy, chose to perpetuate this elegaic tone in his Highland novels – all the sadder since one of the great Gaelic poets, **Duncan Ban Macintyre**, a veteran of the Hanoverian army of 1745, lived in Edinburgh until 1812; his work displaying the true qualities of the finest gaelic poetry: subtlety and keen-eyed observation. Macintyre is buried in Greyfriars churchyard *(18)*.

Scott was trained as a lawyer, and it is worth highlighting the importance of the legal profession to Edinburgh's intellectual life. Following the Union, the court and the parliament were lost, but Scotland kept its seperate legal system. For almost three hundred years, the law has provided one of the few areas of endeavour in which a Scot can reach the top of his profession without leaving Scotland. Important figures who were trained in the law include not only Scott, but **Henry Mackenzie, Lord Cockburn, Lord Kames, James Boswell, David Hume, John Gibson Lockhart** (Scott's son-in-law and biographer) and **Francis Jeffrey**.

The latter two were both involved in Edinburgh's great literary journals of the early 19th century: Jeffrey as co-founder of the Whig *Edinburgh Review*, and Lockhart as an acerbic contributor to the Tory *Blackwood's Magazine*.

The greatest Edinburgh author of the late 19th century was **Robert Louis Stevenson**, who was born in Howard Pl *(6)* in 1850, and who later lived in Heriot Row *(10)*, while being educated at Edinburgh Academy. His boyhood haunts included the villages of Colinton *(22)* and Swanston *(27)*, while, in later years, he spent much time exploring the dark corners of the Old Town. For all that, Edinburgh rarely appears in his books, although *The Strange Case of Dr Jekyll and Mr Hyde* was partly based on the story of Deacon Brodie: the 18th-century Edinburgh city councillor and businessman, who financed his gambling by night-time burglary, and who was hanged in 1788.

A near contemporary of Stevenson was **Sir Arthur Conan Doyle**, who was born in Picardy Pl *(12)*, and lived for some years in George Sq *(19)*. Doyle studied medicine at Edinburgh University, and based his most famous character, Sherlock Holmes, on one of his teachers, Dr Joseph Bell.

The Pentlands: Description

The Pentlands – a narrow line of hills, running about 20 miles (32km) south-west from the southern edge of Edinburgh – are easily reached from the city, and provide some of the finest low-level hill walking in Scotland. The range is criss-crossed by numerous footpaths and tracks *(see p. xiii)* through a variety of landscapes, providing fine views over Lothian, Edinburgh and the Firth of Forth. All the Rights of Way and generally accepted footpaths through the hills are described in this book, and shown on the route maps. Most of the routes described are lineal, but circuits can easily be made by joining routes together. Some alternative shorter loops are described in another book in this series, *Walk Lothian. the Borders & Fife*.

At the northern end of the range, the hills are grassy and steep sided; rising in a cluster of peaks above Edinburgh's southern suburbs. The twin gables of Allermuir and Caerketton *(27)*, scarred by scree and the ski-slopes at Hillend, are familiar landmarks. To the south, the hills divide around the valley of the Logan Burn. The hills to the east are the more dramatic: a line of five pointed peaks between Flotterstone and Eastside Glen, including Scald Law, the highest point in the range at 1899ft/ 579m *(34)*.

 South-west of West Kip, the grass gives way to heather, and the hills begin to subside into the low moorland behind Dunsyre *(40)* and the farmland around Newbigging and Carnwath.

The width of the range varies from four to six miles (6.5-9.5km), with the western slopes gentler than those to the east, where a pronounced fault line has created a straight, steep edge to the ridge of hills.

The greater part of the Pentlands is sandstone, but the more pronounced northern hills, plus the five peaks to the south-east of the Logan Burn, are composed of volcanic rocks. When the hills were covered by ice, during the last Ice Age, the sandstone was more heavily eroded than the harder volcanic rocks, although all the hills bear evidence of the passing glaciers. The broad valley of the Logan Burn and the narrow meltwater channel of Green Cleuch *(both 33)* are typical examples of glacial erosion.

Along the edge of the hills, and in the valleys which cut into the centre of the range, the land is given over to farming: a mixture of arable and grazing, with the fields interrupted by windbreaks and small woods. Most of the remainder of the land is open – grassland to the north, and moorland to the south – with some forestry, mainly on the bleaker, western slopes, as at Boston Cottage *(40)* and Harperrig. The open land is used for sheep-grazing, while the higher slopes are maintained as grouse moors, and parts of the northern end of the range are used by the Army for target practice and other training exercises *(see p. xiii)*.

Scattered throughout the hills are 13 reservoirs, mostly constructed as part of the water supplies, past or present, of Edinburgh and other towns around the Pentlands. The largest of these reservoirs are Harperrig *(37)* and Threipmuir *(32)*, on the western side of the hills. There is only one remaining natural loch in the Pentlands: the tiny Crane Loch at the southern end of the hills.

There are a number of farms in the hills, but no large settlements except on the surrounding farmland. To the north are the suburbs of Edinburgh – Colinton *(22)*, Bonaly *(29)*, Oxgangs and Fairmilehead – and between these and the hills, the little cluster of white-washed cottages at Swanston *(27)*. To the east of the hills are the towns of Penicuik and West Linton *(37,38)*, and the smaller villages of Silverburn, Nine Mile Burn *(34,35)*, Carlops *(36)*, Dolphinton and Dunsyre *(40)* while to the south are the towns of Biggar and Carnwath and the village of Newbigging. Towns are far fewer to the west of the Pentlands, and, apart from the tiny village of Auchengray *(39)*, a few miles from the foot of the hills, there are no settlements of note between Carnwath and the minor conurbation of Balerno *(31)*, Currie *(30,31)* and Juniper Green: all independent villges at one time, but now suburbs of greater Edinburgh.

The northern end of the range, as far south as Carlops, has been designated the Pentland Hills Regional Park.

The Pentlands: History

Given the propinquity of these hills to Edinburgh, the hub of a large part of Scottish history, it is perhaps surprising that they have been witness to so little history themselves; but, apart from one small battle, the building of a few forts, castles and roads, and the passing of generations of cattle drovers and other travellers along the roads down either side of the range, or across the hill passes, the Pentlands have remained comparatively tranquil; though, since the 19th century, they have been used increasingly as a place for recreation by the people of Edinburgh.

The earliest evidence of habitation in the Pentlands is provided by the Stone Age burial cairns – notably those on the peaks of Caerketton *(27)*, Carnethy Hill *(34)* and East Cairn Hill, and the Upper and Nether Cairns in the glen behind Mendick Hill *(38)* – while the earliest surviving defensive structures are the Iron Age forts at Lawhead Hill – south-east of Turnhouse Hill *(34)* – and Castlelaw *(28,29)*. These forts were built by the Votadini: one of the tribes of Britons (Welsh-speaking Celts) who inhabited southern Scotland in the 1st century AD. These forts may well have been built in anticipation of the Roman invasion which took place during that century, and seem to have been abandoned after Lothian was annexed to the Roman Empire.

It would certainly have been unwise of the Romans to have left these forts in the hands of the local tribes, as they both overlook the course of the Roman Road which runs up the eastern side of the hills. The construction of this road established one of the main routes south from Edinburgh, and its course is followed, in places, by both the A702 and the old highway, the Old Biggar Road *(35,37,38)*. In the centuries since the Romans built their road, many travellers have followed its route. In the past, this encouraged the establishment of a number of inns and staging posts along the way; the inns at Carlops *(36)* and Nine Mile Burn *(35)* being examples. The latter was then nine miles from Edinburgh; though it should be noted that this is no longer the case – the original measurement was made in Scots miles, which were a little longer than those now used.

After the Romans had left, the area was once again left to the local tribes: the Picts to the north, and the encroaching Angles of Northumbria to the east and south. The name 'Pentland' means 'Pictland', and the hills may well have been a frontier between these two peoples during the 7th and 8th centuries.

In later years, one of the most notable families of the Pentlands were the Sinclairs (or 'St Clairs') of Roslin *(26)*, to the east of the hills. The family (of Norman extraction) owned land in Lothian as early as the 12th century, and eventually inherited the Earldom of Orkney. A popular tradition states that the 14th-century William Sinclair was responsible for the founding of St. Catherine's Chapel in Glencorse. Apparently, Robert the Bruce had unsuccessfully pursued a deer in the hills. He inquired of his companions if any of them thought that their hounds might fare better. William rashly

wagered his head that his hounds, Help and Hold, would capture the beast before it crossed the March Burn, and the king accepted the wager, balancing it with the offer of extensive lands should the hounds prove successful. Unable to back down, William went through with the challenge, which he duly won. In relief and gratitude, he founded the chapel; now submerged under the waters of Glencorse Reservoir *(29,31,33)*. Bruce died in 1329, and his heart was (carried on a crusade by a party led by Sir James Douglas, and including William Sinclair. Both men died on the expedition, fighting the Moors in Spain.

A later Sinclair, again called William, was responsible for the building of Rosslyn Chapel *(26)*. The chapel was begun in 1446, and, though it was never completed, remains one of the finest buildings of the period in Scotland.

The most important historical period for the Pentlands was the 17th century – the time of the Covenanters.

The Covenanters were adherents to the tenets of strict Presbyterianism, and were at odds with Charles I, and later Charles II and James VII, over perceived attempts to force Episcopalian practices on the Scottish church. Rather than submit to this, some ministers led their congregations into the hills to conduct open-air services, or conventicles; a practice which had to be conducted in secrecy, as the Royalist generals of the time administered harsh punishments on those who were caught.

A number of curious sects emerged during this period of religious hysteria, including the Sweet Singers of Borrowstoneness, who climbed into the Pentlands in the winter of 1681 to observe God's destruction of the city of Edinburgh; the date and time of which had been foretold to their leader in a dream. Fortunately he had been misinformed.

In November of 1666, a group of around 900 Covenanters from the South West of Scotland marched towards Edinburgh, where they hoped to gain support for a general uprising.

The army reached Edinburgh, but failed to find the support it needed, and turned back towards Clydesdale, only to find the way blocked by Sir Thomas Dalyell of the Binns, one of the most vigorous and feared of the Royalist leaders, with an army of some 3000. The Covenanters moved across the northern end of the hills, then marched south . Meanwhile, Dalyell had led his men from Currie, through Maiden's Cleuch *(31)*, and down Glencorse *(31,33)*, and met the Covenanters at Rullion Green, a little to the south of Flotterstone *(33)*. In the resulting battle, some 50 of the Covenanters were killed, and 150 were taken prisoner; 120 to be deported to the West Indies and 30 to be hanged.

There is a monument on the site of the battle, and a stone near the peak of Black Law *(39)*. This latter marks the grave of one of the Covenanters, who was injured in the battle, and died whilst struggling to get home to Ayrshire. He was buried by the farmer from Blackhill Farm, which is now a ruin above Medwynhead *(38)*.

This uncharacteristically violent chapter of Pentland history proved fascinating to Robert Louis Stevenson, who often walked in the hills when he was living in Swanston *(27)*, and whose first published work was a record of the battle, entitled *The Pentland Rising*, which he wrote when he was 16.

The Pentlands: Advice to Walkers

The map below shows the Pentland Hills, the major roads and towns around them, the whereabouts of inns, garages and car parks, and the routes of the footpaths through the hills, numbered as in the book. The way to the start of each route, for those who are driving, is generally simple. For starting points to the east of the hills, follow the signs from the centre of Edinburgh for the A702 to Biggar; for those to the west, follow the signs for the A70 to Lanark. The distance of each of the towns and villages from the centre of Edinburgh is shown on the map.

The starting points are generally easy to find (relevant road and right of way signposts are shown on the map), but one or two require a little navigation. These are listed below.

A Dreghorn *(28)*: drive south from the city centre, as if for the A702, to Fairmilehead. Turn right at the main junction, onto Oxgangs Rd. Turn left from this onto Redford Rd, then left again, at the roundabout, towards the city bypass. Follow the signs for the Forth Road Bridge, but turn left just before joining the bypass, on the minor road to Dreghorn Ranges.

B Swanston *(27)*: drive south from the city centre, as if for the A702, to Fairmilehead. Turn right at the main junction, onto Oxgangs Rd, then left, up Swanston Rd.

C West Linton, golf club *(38)*: to reach the road for the golf club, drive south along the A702 to the west end of West Linton, and then turn right, up Medwyn Rd. The golf club road is the first turn to the left.

D Dunsyre *(40)*: Drive south from the city to Dolphinton, on the A702, then turn right at the sign for Dunsyre. The route is signposted at subsequent junctions. To reach Easton Farm, drive up the minor road beside Dunsyre Mains Farm, but please note that this is a narrow road, and parking is very restricted.

E Balerno *(31,32,36)*: drive south from the city along the A70 and turn left, into Balerno. For Harlaw Reservoir *(31,32)*, turn left up Bavelaw Rd, then left again, up Harlaw Rd. Turn right up the rough road opposite Harlaw Farm to reach the car park. For Threipmuir *(32)*, follow Bavelaw Rd up to the car park at its conclusion, just before the reservoir. For Buteland *(36)*, ignore Bavelaw Rd and carry straight on at the roundabout in Balerno, along Johnsburn Rd. Turn right along Cockburnhill Rd, and follow it to the small car park at the end of the drive into Listonshiels.

F Bonaly *(28,29)*: drive out from the city centre towards the A70, but, before crossing the bypass, turn left along Gillespie Rd to Colinton. At the far end of Colinton, turn back hard right, along Woodhall Rd, then left, up Bonaly Rd, to the car park. Bonaly can also be reached on foot from Colinton, by walking to the east end of the village and turning right, up Dreghorn Loan. At the top of the road, walk on, along the drive of Laverockdale House, then follow the footpath beyond, under the

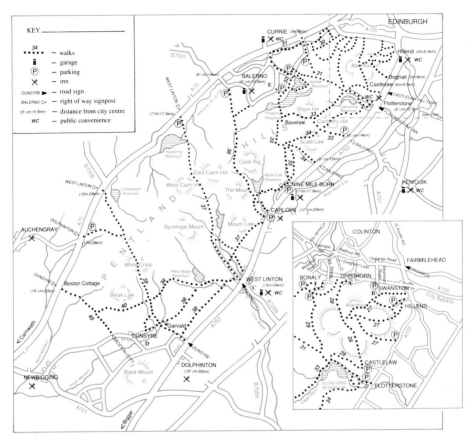

bypass. From the far side there is a choice. To reach the route to Castlelaw *(28)*, cut half left across the field ahead; to reach Bonaly, follow the path which starts along the Bonaly Burn (see map for *29*).

Where a parking sign is shown on the map, a public car park is available. Where a sign is not shown, there is no car park. Parking may be possible along the road verges, but you are asked to keep all roads and gateways clear for farm vehicles, and to try and use the car parks whenever possible.

When you are walking in the hills, you are asked to stick to the footpaths. These are generally clear in the northern half of the hills, but become less obvious to the south. You are advised to take a

large scale map with you on all countryside walks but, in particular, on the walks in the southern part of the hills *(36,37,38,39,40)*, and also on any of the longer routes in the north. The Bartholomew *Pentland Hills Walking Map* is ideal.

The walks in the Pentlands are not particularly dangerous, but you are asked to take care when on the hills. Wear stout footwear, and take waterproof clothing and something to eat and drink. On the longer routes, check the weather forecast before going, carry a compass and make sure that someone knows where you have gone.

Grouse shooting takes place between 12th Aug and 10th Dec. During the remainder of the year there is no danger in walking across the moors, and the lines of butts across favoured slopes are a feature of several of the routes, but **for this period some discretion should be shown, and areas where shooting is clearly in progress should be avoided.**

Parts of the northern end of the range are used by the Army for target practice and other training exercises *(28,29)*. **When red flags are flown near the paths through these areas, you are asked to keep out, for your own safety. You are also asked not to pick up any strange objects found along these routes, as they may be explosive.**

Much of the Pentland Hills is given over to sheep grazing. On the Contents Page, the Pentland walks are shown as being suitable for dogs, but there is an important rider to this: **all dogs must be kept under strict control when passing through grazing areas.** Some farmers have erected signs threatening to shoot animals seen sheep-worrying, and it is hard not to sympathise.

It is possible to make circuits by joining the routes across the hills with sections along major and minor public roads *(see maps)*. Wherever possible, try and avoid the A702; there are pavements along part of the road, but it is very busy. The A70 is quieter.

If you have any questions about access to the hills, get in touch with the Pentland Ranger Service at Hillend *(27)* or Flotterstone *(33)*; telephone 445 3383. Assistance with questions about public transport can be obtained from the Edinburgh Tourist Information Centre; telephone (031) 557 1700.

Natural History

The walks through the centre of Edinburgh are of interest for their architecture rather than their natural history, but the route through the extensive Botanic Gardens *(6)* is of great interest, while the Union Canal *(21,25)* and Water of Leith *(5,6,7,8)* provide a habitat for **coot, moorhen** and **ducks**. These routes also pass extensive areas of deciduous woodland, as do other riverside and woodland walks around and outside the city *(1,2,4,22,23,24,26)*, providing a habitat for **great, blue** and **coal tits, treecreeper, wren, great-spotted** and **green woodpeckers, woodcock** and **woodpigeon**, plus the **tawny owl** and a variety of **finches** and **warblers**, while the **grey squirrel** is very common, even in Princes Street Gardens *(14,17)*. Wooded glens throughout the area *(2,4,7,8,20,21,22,23,25,26,30)* encourage **dipper, heron** and **grey** and **pied wagtails**.

In the more open, low-lying areas *(1,4,20,23, 25-40)*, **yellowhammer, wheatear, linnet** and **spotted flycatcher** may be seen, plus **pheasant**, and **partridge**, while **swift, swallow** and **house** and **sand martins** circle overhead.

The largest block of rural routes are those in the Pentland Hills *(27-40)*. The greater part of the range is given over to open grassland and moorland of **ling** and **bell heather**. These areas provide a habitat for **red** and **black grouse**, and also for waders such as **lapwing, curlew, snipe** and **redshank**, plus the ubiquitous **meadow pipit** and the **skylark**. Birds of prey include the **kestrel** and the day-hunting **short-eared owl**. Scavanging **crows** may be seen on the moors and, indeed, throughout the area, while the **magpie** will be found in the lower farmland. The **mountain hare**, which turns white during the winter, can occasionally be found on the high ground, while the larger **brown hare** is present in the farmland. **Fox, roe deer, weasel, stoat** and **rabbit** are all present in the hills, though they are unlikely to be seen.

Woodland is not plentiful in the hills, though there is some forestry *(29,40)*, consisting largely of conifers, and a number of small plantations, wind breaks and field boundaries on the lower ground.

The reservoirs in the Pentlands *(29,31,32,33,36,37)* encourage a number of freshwater birds, including **coot, moorhen, cormorant** and **great-crested grebe**, plus **mallard, wigeon, teal, tufted duck, goldeneye** and **red-breasted merganser**, and **greylag** and **pink-footed geese**. The greatest density of freshwater birds can be found at the Bavelaw Marsh Nature Reserve, at the western end of Threipmuir Reservoir *(32)*.

1 Queensferry to Cramond

Length: 4 miles (6.5km) one way
Height climbed: None
Grade: C
Public conveniences: Queensferry; Cramond
Public transport: Bus service linking city centre,
Barnton and Queensferry (see text)

A lineal path through coastal farmland and woodland, linking two historic villages. A short ferry trip is required, so take money.

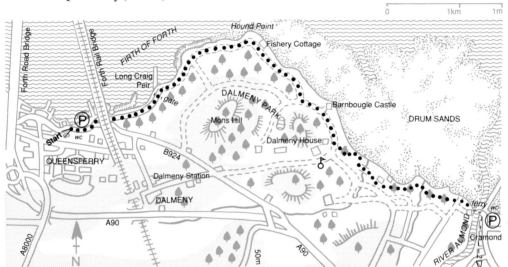

This route runs between a small town and a village on the southern shore of the Firth of Forth. There is no bus service between the two settlements, but it is possible to return to the start by following *Walk 2* from Cramond to Barnton and catching a Queensferry bus from there (bus stop shown on *Walk 2* map). Obviously, the route can be walked either way.

To start from Queensferry, drive west from the city along the A90, and turn left at the signs for the town, which is about nine miles (14.5km) from the city centre.

Queensferry is a fine town, with a splendid main street and a long history as a ferry terminus. The ferry is gone now, and the town is squeezed between the massive supports of the Forth Rail Bridge (completed 1890) and the Forth Road Bridge (1964).

Park in the town and walk eastwards along the

front, towards the Rail Bridge. Just before it is reached, a tarmac road cuts off to the left. Follow this under the bridge and on to Long Craig Pier, where there is a gate, and a sign noting the fare (minimal) and operating hours of the ferry which links the far end of the walk with Cramond.

The route beyond the gate is quite clear; running through woodland and farmland, giving fine views of the firth, and passing two large houses: Barnbougle Castle (largely 17th-century, but renovated in the 19th) and Dalmeny House (1815; home of the Earls of Rosebery). At Dalmeny, walk round the front edge of the golf course in front of the house to reach a footbridge over the small burn beyond; then continue for a mile (1.5km) to the narrow mouth of the River Almond, where (if you have checked the times correctly) the ferryman will scull you across the river to the whitewashed village of Cramond.

2 Cramond

Length: 4 miles (6.5km)
Height climbed: 100ft (30m)
Grade: C
Public conveniences: Cramond
Public transport: Bus service between city centre
and Barnton (see map)

*Good footpaths leading from a fine coastal
village, by the mouth of a river, up a narrow,
wooded glen.*

Cramond is a picturesque little coastal village of
whitewashed 18th-century terraces, clustered
around the mouth of the River Almond. It has a
long history, dating back to Roman times, when a
fort was established on the site. Remaining old
buildings in the village include the church (largely
17th century) and Cramond Tower (15th century).

To reach the village by car, drive west from the
centre of the city on the Queensferry Rd. At the
Barnton Roundabout turn right, down Whitehouse
Rd. Park in the village car park and walk down to
the river. From the mouth of the river, a causeway
runs out across the Drum Sands to tiny Cramond
Island. This is a pleasant walk, but the causeway is
tidal and **it is dangerous to cross except at certain
periods. These are shown on a board by the
causeway.** There is also a ferry across the mouth
of the River Almond, linking Cramond with a
coastal footpath to Queensferry *(Walk 1)*.

For this route, however, walk up the river bank,
out of the village. There is a clear track running a
little over a mile (1.5km) from the village to the
Cramond Old Brig (early 16th century), which is
dwarfed by the new road bridge behind it. The
track runs through mixed woodland in a shallow
gorge, and the various weirs, ruined mills and rows
of workmen's cottages are evidence of the
Almond's importance as an early industrial site.

From the near end of the old bridge, follow the
footpath (signposted for Cammo) which leads on
up the river bank, under the road bridge and on
through woodland. Just after the path crosses a
very small burn, it cuts up to the left, between
houses, to join a tarmac road. Turn right along this.
At the end of the houses, turn right again, down a
clear footpath which leads along the river to
another bridge. Cross this and return down the far
side of the river, back under the road bridge and
across the Old Brig to return by the original track.

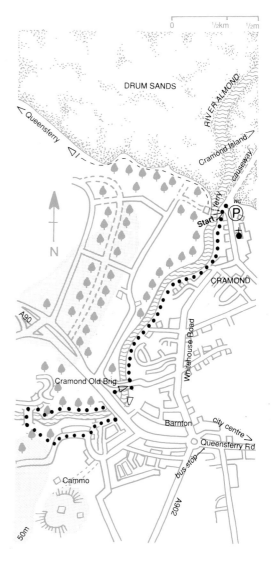

3 Leith

Length: 2 miles (3km)
Height climbed: None
Grade: C
Public conveniences: See map
Public transport: Bus services between city centre
and Leith

*A walk through the buildings and parks of the
historic port of Leith.*

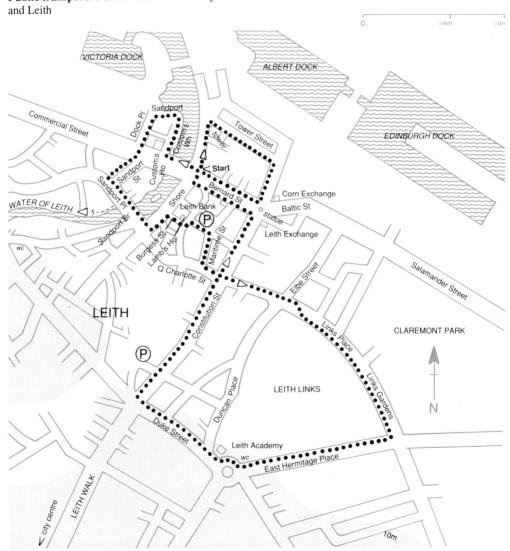

Edinburgh is unusual amongst the capitals of Europe in that its centre is neither on the coast nor by a large river. The reason lies in the very antiquity of the city, which began to develop as a settlement around successive forts and castles on Edinburgh Rock, well before the period when sea-borne trade was considered more important than defence.

When trade did start to develop, it was handled by the separate burgh of Leith, situated two and a half miles (4km) from Edinburgh Castle, at the point where the Water of Leith debouches into the Firth of Forth.

Edinburgh gradually spread towards its smaller neighbour, but the port of Leith retained its independence until 1920, and even now – when the port is completely engulfed by greater Edinburgh – it retains its own identity.

For many years the town was rather neglected but, recently, great efforts have been made to tidy up the old buildings, and to improve the quality of the new building being undertaken, and there is now much of interest to be seen.

Leith can be reached by bus or car (drive down Leith Walk from the east end of Princes St; there is generally room to park in the streets near the docks), or by foot *(Walk 5)*. Once in the town, make for the junction of Bernard St and Shore, on the eastern side of the Water of Leith, and start walking from there.

Walk down Shore, with the river to the left; passing the spot where George IV landed when he visited Edinburgh in 1822 (to be met by Walter Scott, who was largely responsible for the ceremonies surrounding the royal visit). Ships may be visible ahead in Leith docks, though, curiously, there is little feeling in the town that it is a major sea-port.

Turn right into Tower St, with the signal tower (Robert Mylne, 1685; originally a windmill) up to the right on the corner. This is an area of warehousing, and there is often a strong smell of fish about the street.

At the end of the street, turn right, into Constitution St. Walk up the right-hand side of the street to a large junction, with a statue of Robert Burns in the centre of the road. To the left, at this point, is the old Corn Exchange building (1860), while ahead and to the left, on the far side of the junction, is the Leith Exchange building (Thomas Brown, 1809). Turn right, into Bernard St, noting the old Leith bank (1804), with its low dome, on the far side of the street. When the street reaches Shore, walk across it, and on across the bridge over the river beyond, and then turn right down Customs Wharf, just before the impressive Customs House (Robert Reid, 1812). Continue along the Sandport, with the basin to the right and new housing to the left, then cut left around the end of the housing, then left again, through it, up to Dock Pl and on to Commercial St.

On the far side of the street is an open, grassy area, with a path running through it, parallel to the terrace beside Sandport St, to the left. Cross Commercial St and follow this path up to Sandport Pl, then cut left, across Sandport Bridge.

At the far end, turn left down the right-hand side of Shore, then turn right along Burgess St. Walk to the junction at the end of the street, then turn left around Lamb's House – a white-harled merchant's house of the early 17th century. Carry on until a car park appears to the right, and cut right before it, along the front of the new flats at Maritime Court, then right again, up Maritime St. Continue up this street until it reaches a T junction, then turn left, along Queen Charlotte St. When the street reaches Constitution St cross it and continue beyond; crossing the end of Elbe Street and continuing along Links Pl. Cross to the right-hand side of the road and continue, with Leith Links to the right, and the buildings to the left eventually giving way to Claremont Park.

When the road reaches a junction, turn right up East Hermitage Pl, and continue along this road, with 19th century housing to the left and the Links to the right. At the junction head half right, across the face of Leith Academy and the end of Duncan Pl, and on down Duke St. Continue on this road until the next main junction, and then turn right down Constitution St. Walk down the left-hand side of the street and then, when it reaches the junction around the Burns statue, turn left along Bernard St to return to the start of the walk.

4 Musselburgh

Length: 6 miles (9.5km)
Height climbed: Negligible
Grade: B
Public conveniences: Musselburgh; Fisherrow
Public transport: Bus services between city centre
and Musselburgh

*A walk through pleasant farmland and
woodland by a river-bank, plus a section
along the estuary coast, and diversions
through Fisherrow and Musselburgh.*

Some six miles (9.5km) east of the centre of
Edinburgh, the River Esk flows into the Firth of
Forth, and about the mouth of the Esk are the towns
of Fisherrow to the west and Musselburgh to the
east. As their names suggest, both settlements were
once fishing harbours.

To reach the start of the walk by car, drive
north from the city centre to Leith, then east on the
A199. Turn left into Fisherrow and park in the car
park by the small harbour. Walk east from the
harbour along the Promenade and, when the
buildings finish, continue with Fisherrow Links to
the right, until the path reaches the River Esk.

Turn right, along a path by the riverside.
Follow this past two footbridges (a short detour
across the second leads to Musselburgh town
centre) and under a road bridge; then cross the old
bridge and continue up the river. At the next road
bridge, cross the road and look for a sign for the
River Esk Walkway. This leads to a path up the
left-hand side of the river; through an industrial
estate, and then on, through woodland and
farmland by the riverside. Leave the path after
about two miles (3km), just after it is crossed by
the bypass. A tarmac road heads left, leading to the
A6124. Turn left along this, over the bypass and
on into the pleasant village of Inveresk. The
gardens of Inveresk Lodge, to the left of the road,
are open to the public.

At the end of the village the road splits. Go
left, down the road signposted as a dead-end. To
the right, at the end of the road, is St. Michael's
Church (1805); while to the left a track leads back
down to the path by the river. Retrace your steps
along this path back into Musselburgh and walk
down to the lower of the two road bridges. Cross
this and follow Bridge St and North High St
beyond until Harbour Rd cuts right, leading back
to the start of the route.

5 Water of Leith Walkway

Length: 4 miles (6.5km)
Height climbed: Negligible
Grade: C
Public conveniences: See map
Public transport: Numerous city bus services

A walk through the fine architecture of the eastern New Town, plus a footpath by the Water of Leith. Back by Leith Walk.

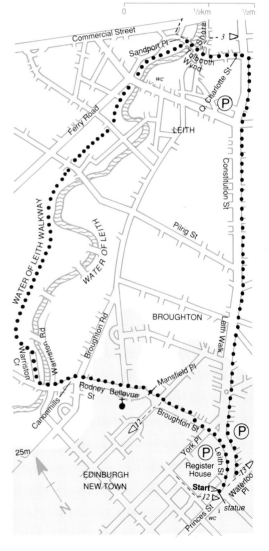

Start from the equestrian statue of Wellington at the eastern end of Princes St *(see p. i)*, in front of Register House (Robert Adam, started 1774), and walk down the left-hand side of Leith St, with the modern St. James shopping centre to the left. At the major roundabout keep left, cross the end of York Pl and walk down Broughton St. At the roundabout keep straight on, down Mansfield Pl, Bellevue – notice Bellevue Cr to the left (1802) and the fine St. Mary's Church in its centre (Thomas Brown, 1826) – and Rodney St to a further junction. Continue straight on beyond this, down the right-hand side of Canonmills; crossing the end of Warriston Rd and the Water of Leith before turning right along the terrace of Warriston Cr (1818). At the end of the road there is a sign indicating a footpath to Leith.

Follow this path, which climbs onto a disused railway line. Turn left along this and continue on the clear track beyond, between high walls and then through a mixture of housing and open ground towards Leith. It is a little over a mile (1.5km) from Warriston to Leith, and along the latter part of the path the Water of Leith – broadening as it nears the sea – flows beside the path.

When the path ends, turn right along Sandport Pl, over the bridge. At the junction with Shore, either turn left, to reach the start of *Walk 3*, or carry straight on, along Tolbooth Wynd and Queen Charlotte St, to reach Constitution St. Turn right up this and, at the main junction, carry straight on, along Leith Walk – the old main road linking Edinburgh with its port of Leith. Note the fine Smith's Pl (1812), a short way up the road on the left.

Keep to the left all the way up the road and carry straight on at the two roundabouts, into Leith St. Continue up this until its junction with Waterloo Pl, then cut right, across the top of the street, to return to the start of the walk.

6 Royal Botanic Gardens

Length: 1¹/₂ miles (2.5km), plus Botanic Gardens
Height climbed: Negligible
Grade: C
Public conveniences: See map
Public transport: Numerous city bus services

A walk through New Town terraces and along footpaths by the Water of Leith, leading to the splendid Royal Botanic Gardens.

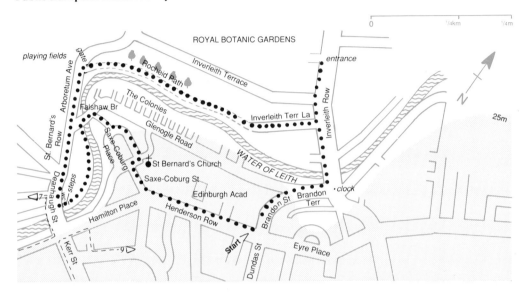

Start from the bottom of Dundas St *(see p. i)* and walk westwards along the right-hand side of Henderson Row, passing Edinburgh Academy to the right (William Burn, 1823-36). This was the school attended by Robert Louis Stevenson.

As the road bends to the left, into Hamilton Pl, turn right, up Saxe-Coburg St. Pass St. Bernard's Church (James Milne, 1823) and continue into Saxe-Coburg Pl (terraced houses by Milne, 1822, and Adam Turnbull, 1828). The crescent at the far end of the place was never completed, and a tarmac path now runs through the gap. Follow this down to Glenogle Rd, noting the rows of terraced artisans' flats below (Edinburgh Co-operative Building Company, 1861) known as the 'Colonies'.

Turn left along Glenogle Rd and then Bridge Pl, crossing the Falshaw Bridge over the Water Of Leith. At the far end of the bridge, turn left up the waterside footpath. Follow this to the next bridge

across the river and climb the steps to the right. Turn right, along Deanhaugh St, then right again, up St. Bernard's Row. As the road approaches Falshaw Bridge again, turn half-left, up Arboretum Ave.

Follow this road, with playing fields to the left and the Water of Leith beyond a fence to the right, and the Colonies beyond that, until there is a gate to the right, leading to the start of the Rocheid Path: a clear track through a wooded slope above the river.

Follow this track, and the garage-lined Inverleith Terrace Lane beyond, to Inverleith Row, then turn left, crossing the end of Inverleith Terrace and continuing to the entrance to the Royal Botanic Gardens.

To return, double back down Inverleith Row to a junction around a clock. Turn right, into Brandon Terr, then continue up Brandon St, back to the start.

7 Dean Village

Length: 2 miles (3km)
Height climbed: Undulating
Grade: C
Public conveniences: See *p. i*
Public transport: Numerous city bus services

A walk through an old mill village, along some of the finest New Town terraces, and through a picturesque wooded glen; passing Dean Village, the Water of Leith and Ann St.

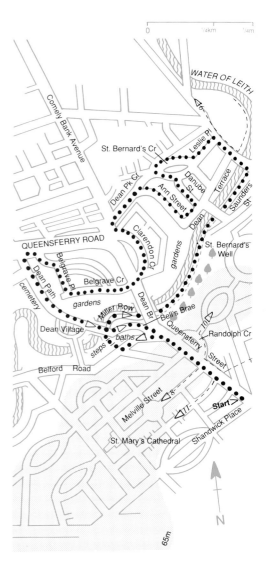

Start at the end of Queensferry St, near the west end of Princes St *(see p. i)*, and walk up its left-hand side until, just before it crosses the Dean Bridge, Belford Rd swings off to the left. Follow this until, just beyond the Drumsheugh Baths building (1888), a flight of steps leads down to the right, signposted 'Belford Rd 10-11'. Walk down these steps, noting the view of Dean Village ahead. Cross Bells Brae and walk on along Miller Row, with the Water of Leith to the left.

Continue along this clear path, under a high arch of the Dean Bridge (Thomas Telford, 1832) and on, with a wooded bank to the right, to St. Bernard's Well – a mineral spring, topped with an elegant Doric folly (Alexander Nasmyth, 1789). Follow either of the two paths beyond to the next bridge, pass beneath it and continue along Saunders St, with modern housing to the right.

Turn left across the next bridge and continue up the road beyond. Cross the end of Dean Terrace and then turn left into Leslie Pl. When the road splits, veer right into the terraced St. Bernard's Cr (James Milne, 1824), then hard left round the central garden and right down Danube St. At the foot of the street turn right, along Dean Terrace, then swing right into the splendid Ann St (James Milne, 1814).

At the end of the street turn left, up Dean Park Cr, then left again, along Clarendon Cr (John Tait, 1850-53). At the end of the crescent turn right, across Queensferry Rd, and carry straight on down Belgrave Cr (1874). Near the end of the terrace turn right, into Belgrave Pl, from which there is a marvellous view of chateau-like Fettes College (David Bryce, 1862-70).

When the road reaches Queensferry Rd turn left, then double back, up Dean Path. Continue down into Dean Village, across the bridge, then up Bells Brae to rejoin Queensferry St.

8 West End

Length: 2 miles (3km)
Height climbed: Undulating
Grade: C
Public conveniences: See *p. i*
Public transport: Numerous city bus services

A walk through the terraces and crescents of the western New Town, plus a footpath through a picturesque, wooded glen. Passing Melville St, the Water of Leith and the Gallery of Modern Art.

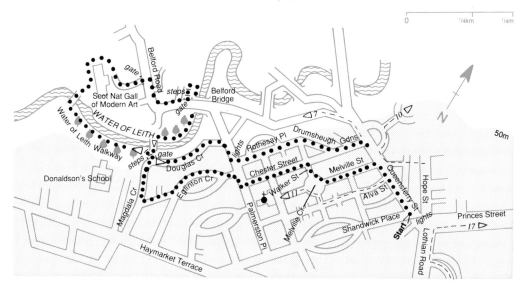

Start at the end of Queensferry St, near the west end of Princes St *(see p. i)* and walk up its left-hand side. Turn left into Melville St (1820-60), noticing St. Mary's Cathedral (completed 1879) at the far end of the street.

Turn right at Melville Cr, up Walker St, then turn left along Chester St. At the far end of the street cross Palmerston Pl, then turn right for a short distance before turning left down Eglinton Cr. When the road splits, stay to the right. Continue until the road joins Magdala Cr, then turn right, noting Donaldson's School (Playfair, 1842-54) through the trees to the left.

At the curve in the road, where Douglas Cr joins from the east, cut left, through a gate, and follow a flight of steps, signposted 'Water of Leith Walkway', down to the river.

Turn left at the bottom, along a clear track, with the river to the right and a bank of trees to the left.

When the trees end, continue for a short distance until a bridge appears over the river. Cross this and climb the path opposite, leading up to the Scottish National Gallery of Modern Art. Walk round to the left of the gallery and follow its driveway down to Belford Rd. **NB: outside gallery opening hours (Mon-Sat 10-5; Sun 2-5) this loop of the walk is not possible.**

Follow the road until, just before it crosses the river, there is a gateway to the left and a flight of steps leading down to the water. Turn right along the path, under Belford Bridge, across the river and back to the steps from Magdala Cr. Climb these, then turn left, along Douglas Cr. At the end turn right, into Palmerston Pl. Carry on until the crossing point is reached, cross the road and double back to turn into Rothesay Pl. At the end of the place turn half right into Drumsheugh Gdns. Follow this till it joins Queensferry St.

9 Royal Circus

Length: 1¹/₂ miles (2.5km)
Height climbed: Negligible
Grade: C
Public conveniences: See map
Public transport: Numerous city bus services

A walk through some of the finest architecture of the northern New Town; passing the elegant terraces of Royal Circus, Moray Pl, Stockbridge, Royal Cr and Drummond Pl.

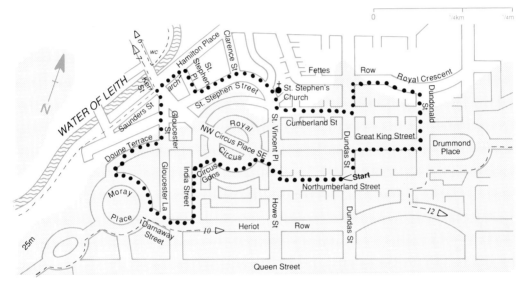

Start from the junction of Northumberland St and Dundas St *(see p. i)*. Walk west along the right-hand side of Northumberland St. At the end of the street, turn right up Howe St. Cross this at the crossing place and turn up South East Circus Pl, then left, into Royal Circus (Playfair, 1821-23). At the end of the terrace, turn left, up Circus Gdns, then left again, up the right-hand side of India St (development started 1819).

At the top of India St turn right along Heriot Row, then across the head of Gloucester Lane and on down Darnaway St to Moray Pl (James Gillespie Graham, 1822-27). Turn right, then first right, down Doune Terrace (part of the same development), with gardens to the left; then turn left, down the left-hand side of Gloucester St.

At the foot of the street, veer left for a short distance, along Kerr St, then cross this at the first junction and walk along Hamilton Pl opposite, with

the Water of Leith to the left. After a short distance turn right, through an arch, into St Stephen Pl. This was the site of the Stockbridge Market, which operated from 1825-1900.

Walk through the upper arch and on to St. Stephen St, then turn left. Follow this road as it curves up to the right, to its conclusion at the massive St. Stephen's Church (Playfair, 1828). Turn left beyond the church: across the foot of St. Vincent St and down Cumberland St (originally built to house artisans). At the end of the street cross Dundas St and turn left, for a short distance, then right, along Fettes Row, to Royal Cr (1819-88).

From the middle of Royal Cr turn right, up Dundonald St, to Drummond Pl (mostly 1818 onwards); then turn right, into the splendid Great King St (Robert Reid, 1817). Turn left at the first junction to return to the start.

10 George Street

Length: 1¹/₂ miles (2.5km)
Height climbed: Negligible
Grade: C
Public conveniences: See map
Public transport: Numerous city bus services

A walk through the heart of the New Town, passing some if its finest streets, squares and terraces, including St. Andrew Sq, George St, Charlotte Sq, Randolph Cr, Moray Pl and Heriot Row.

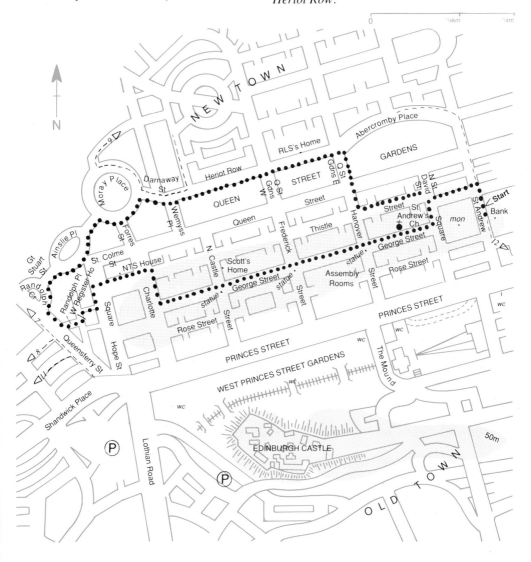

In the mid 18th century Edinburgh was still a mediaeval city, largely confined to the area which is now called the Old Town, clustered around the castle. The resulting overpopulation was uncomfortable and unhealthy, and the Lord Provost, George Drummond, proposed that the city be extended to the north *(see p. v)*. The North Loch (which then filled the area of Princes Street Gardens) was drained, and the North Bridge built across the marshland to the east of it to provide easy access to the farmland beyond. A competition was held to decide on the best design for a New Town, and was won by James Craig – only 23 at the time – with an elegant, symmetrical design (in complete contrast to the Old Town) of two squares linked by a grid of roads. The street and square names symbolised the still recent Union of Scotland and England (Thistle St and Rose St; St. Andrew Sq and St. George Sq – the latter subsequently changed to Charlotte Sq, after Queen Charlotte).

The New Town proved a great success, and by the early 19th century the area defined by Craig, between the two squares and Queen St and Princes St, had been completed.

Start this walk from the eastern side of St. Andrew Sq *(p. i)*, outside the Royal Bank of Scotland building (Sir William Chambers, 1772-74; originally the town house of the Dundas family) and walk round the northern side of the square, noting the central monument to Henry Dundas, 1st Viscount Melville (1822).

From the far side of the square, walk down the right-hand side of George St, passing the oval St. Andrew's Church (1785, spire 1789) to the right, and the statue of George IV at the junction with Hanover St (George IV visited Edinburgh in 1822). Beyond Hanover St, on the far side of the road, are the Assembly Rooms (1818, with later additions) – a two storey classical building, with a three-arched arcade projecting onto the pavement. At one time, this building was the hub of Edinburgh society, and it was here that Sir Walter Scott finally admitted his authorship of the Waverley novels.

Continue across Frederick St, with its statue of Pitt, and on to Castle Street. At this point take a short detour to the right, down North Castle Street.

Number 39 (1790-93; with distinctive shallow bow windows) was the home of Sir Walter Scott from 1802-26.

Continue to the western end of George St, then veer right, to pass round the northern side of Charlotte Sq (Robert Adam, 1791). Number seven is owned by the National Trust for Scotland and is open to the public. It has been restored to represent a typical Edinburgh town house of the late 18th century

Walk round to the west side of the square and down the right-hand side of St George's Church (Robert Reid, 1811; now West Register House), then straight on down Randolph Pl (there is a fine view ahead of St. Mary's Cathedral) to Queensferry St. Turn right, then right again, into Randolph Cr – the most westerly terrace in an area of Edinburgh developed by the Earl of Moray, which also includes Ainslie Pl and Moray Pl (all James Gillespie Graham, 1822-27). Walk half way round the crescent then turn right, down Great Stuart St, to Ainslie Pl. When the road splits go right, across the foot of St. Colme St and on to the extension of Great Stuart St. Follow this into Moray Place (the Earl's town house was number 28) and turn right. Cross the end of Forres St and then turn right into Darnaway St; cross the foot of Wemyss Pl then continue along the right-hand side of Heriot Row, with Queen St Gdns to the right and a fine terrace to the left (Robert Reid, 1801-2). Cross the end of Queen St Gdns West and continue. To the left, a short distance after the junction, is number 17 – home of the author Robert Louis Stevenson from 1857-80.

Turn right up the left-hand side of Queen St Gdns East, passing between the gardens, then cross Queen St and continue up Hanover St. Half way up, turn left into Thistle St. On the right of the street are two small houses facing each other. These are thought to be the two earliest surviving buildings of the New Town, built in 1767.

At the end of the road turn right, up North St. David St, to return to St. Andrew Sq. The name 'St. David St' was an ironic reference to the well-liked but controversial athiest David Hume, who was an early resident in the street.

11 St. Mary's Cathedral

Length: 1 mile (1.5km)
Height climbed: None
Grade: C
Public conveniences: See *p. i*
Public transport: Numerous city bus services

A short walk through the elegant terraces, crescents and squares of the west end of the New Town; passing Melville St, the grand St. Mary's Cathedral, Atholl Cres and Rutland Sq.

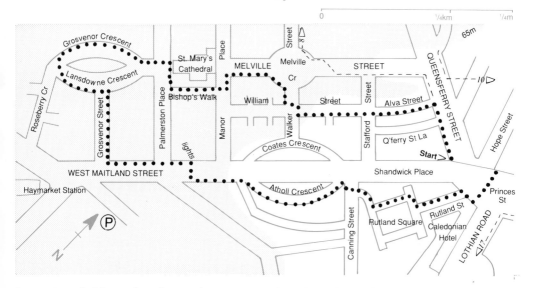

Start at the end of Queensferry St, near the west end of Princes St *(see p. i)* and walk up its left-hand side. Turn left into terraced Alva St, continue across Stafford St into William St (1824-25) then turn right, up Walker St, to Melville Cres (1820-60). Notice the statue of Robert Dundas, 2nd Viscount Melville, in the centre of the square.

Turn left along Melville St, with the elegant St. Mary's Cathedral ahead (Sir George Gilbert Scott, completed 1879), with its three spires. The two smaller spires (at the far end of the building) are named Barbara and Mary, after two daughters of the Walker family who owned and developed this part of the town.

Cross Manor Pl and turn left, then right, along Bishop's Walk, to the left of the cathedral. At the end of the walk turn right, to the main entrance of the cathedral, then cross Palmerston Pl and walk down the road opposite. When this road splits, go right, along the Victorian terrace of Grosvenor Cr. Turn left at the end and double back down Lansdowne Cr, then cut right down Grosvenor St. Cross this and turn left along West Maitland St, pausing to look back to Haymarket Station (1840-42) on the far side of a large junction. Cross West Maitland St at the crossing place and continue, before cutting right, into Atholl Cr (Thomas Bonnar, 1824-25). Notice Coates Cr opposite (Robert Brown, 1813-23).

At the end turn right, into Canning St. Cross this and cut left, into Rutland Sq (Archibald Elliot, 1819). Walk through the square and leave it along Rutland St, with the vast Caledonian Hotel (1898-1902) to the right. Turn left at the end, across Princes St, to return to the start.

12 East New Town

Length: 1½ miles (2.5km)
Height climbed: Negligible
Grade: C
Public conveniences: See map
Public transport: Numerous city bus services

A walk through the elegant squares and terraces of the eastern New Town, passing Adam's splendid Register House, plus Gayfield Sq, Drummond Pl, Abercromby Pl and St. Andrew Sq.

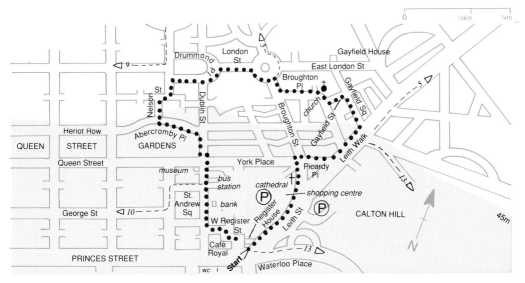

Start from the equestrian statue of Wellington at the eastern end of Princes St *(see p. i)*, in front of the fine Register House (Robert Adam, started 1774), and walk down the left-hand side of Leith St, with the modern St. James shopping centre to the left. When the road reaches a large roundabout keep left, past St. Mary's Roman Catholic Cathedral, and cross the ends of York Pl and Broughton St to join Picardy Pl (Arthur Conan Doyle was born at No 2).

Continue down the left-hand side of Leith Walk before turning left into Gayfield Sq. This was built on the gardens of Gayfield House (1763) – still standing to the north of the square – in 1790. At the far end of the square, turn left into Gayfield St, then turn right, past Broughton Pl Church (1821), into Broughton Pl beyond, with its handsome early 19th-century terraces.

At the end of Broughton Pl turn right into Broughton St, then left at the roundabout into London St and on to Drummond Pl (the last two both planned by Robert Reid in 1801-2). Veer left round the small park at the centre of the place, crossing the foot of Dublin St and turning left up Nelson St to climb up to join Abercromby Pl (1801-2).

Cross the road and turn left, with the elegant terrace to the left and Queen St Gdns to the right.

Turn right up Dublin St, then cross it as it joins Queen St – notice the red block of the National Museum of Antiquities (1886-90) on the opposite corner. Cross Queen St and climb up the left-hand side of North St. Andrew St into St. Andrew Sq. Continue along the east side of the square – passing the Royal Bank of Scotland building (originally the Dundas mansion: Chambers, 1772-74) – before turning left down West Register St; passing the Cafe Royal (1862) and then turning right to return to the start.

13 Calton

Length: 1¹/₂ miles (2.5km)
Height climbed: 130ft (40m)
Grade: C
Public conveniences: See map
Public transport: Numerous city bus services

A walk around the terraces of the eastern New Town, plus a climb up Calton Hill, with its cluster of monuments and fine views over the city; passing Calton Old Burial Ground, the National Monument and Nelson's Monument.

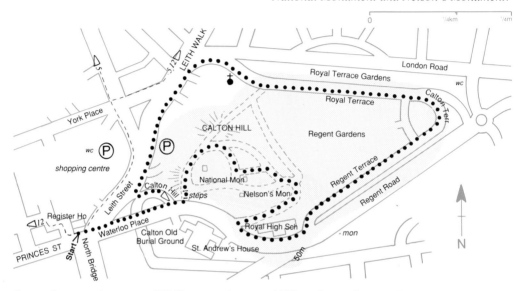

Start at the equestrian statue of Wellington at the east end of Princes St *(see p. i)*; in front of Register House (Robert Adam, started 1774). Cross the top of Leith St and walk on along Waterloo Pl. A short way along the road, to the right, is the entrance to the Calton Old Burial Ground. Amongst those buried here is David Hume *(p. viii)* (beneath a fine monument by Robert Adam, 1778).

Beyond the graveyard looms the art-deco mass of St Andrew's House (1934-39). A short distance before this a flight of steps leads up to the left of the road onto Calton Hill. The hill provides fine views – particularly from the tower of Nelson's Monument (1816), which can be climbed for a small fee. This is only one of a curious assortment of buildings and monuments clustered about the summit, including the Old Observatory (James Craig, 1776), the New Observatory (Playfair, 1818), Dugald Stewart's Monument (Playfair,

1832), and, most famous of all, the National Monument (Cockerell/Playfair, 1822): a copy of the Parthenon intended as a memorial of the Napoleonic Wars. Only twelve columns were ever built, due to a lack of funds. **(Warning: don't walk on the hill at night.)**

A possible route over the hill is shown on the map, but there are any number of paths and tracks. Return to Regent Rd and turn left, past the old Royal High School building (Thomas Hamilton, 1825-29), then veer left up Regent Terr (Playfair, 1819). Notice the monument to Robert Burns a short distance beyond the junction (1830).

At the end of the terrace follow the curve round Calton Terr and then walk on down Royal Terr (both Playfair). At the end of the road turn left, up Leith walk, then, opposite the modern St. James Centre, turn up Calton Hill before dropping back down to Waterloo Pl.

14 Edinburgh Castle

Length: 1¹/₂ miles (2.5km)
Height climbed: Steeply undulating
Grade: C
Public conveniences: See map
Public transport: Numerous city bus services

A steep walk around the narrow streets of the Old Town and along Princes St, passing Edinburgh Castle, the National Gallery, the Royal Scottish Academy, the Scott Monument, East Princes St Gdns and the Lawnmarket.

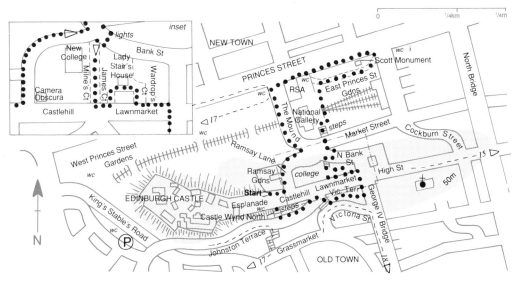

Start from the Esplanade before the entrance to the castle (*see p. i*), with its fine views of Edinburgh, the Firth of Forth and the Pentland Hills.

Walk down Castlehill and turn left down Ramsay La, just before the crenellated Camera Obscura building. Note the splendid Ramsay Gdns (Patrick Geddes, 1892-3) to the left, and the stark New College (Playfair, 1846-50), with its two square towers, beyond to the right. At the foot of the lane turn left, down the Mound, with the neo-Classical temples of the National Gallery (Playfair, 1845) and the Royal Scottish Academy (Playfair, 1822-26) to the right, to the junction with Princes St. Cut right, across the Mound and along the near side of Princes St, with East Princes St Gdns to the right. Continue past the tall Scott Monument (George Meikle Kemp, 1844), then turn right again, after a short distance, into the gardens.

Walk back through the gardens towards the National Gallery, then climb the steps and cut left, up the Playfair Steps to the Mound. Cross the end of Market St, and Bank St beyond, then cut right, back to the New College, and climb the steps leading to Milnes Court on its near side. Climb up through the court to the Lawnmarket, then turn left, then left again, into the West Entry of James Court. Turn right and walk to the far end of the court (passing the literary museum at Lady Stair's House), then cut right, through Wardrop's Court, and turn left down to the junction.

Cross the Lawnmarket and walk down George IV Bridge, with the modern Lothian Regional Council building (1970) to the right. At the end of the building cut right, up some steps, onto Victoria Terr. Follow the terrace to its end, then cut right, up the steps, and cross Johnston Terr. Turn left for a short distance, then climb the steps of Castle Wynd North to return to the Esplanade.

15 High Street

Length: 1½ miles (2.5km)
Height climbed: Steeply undulating
Grade: C
Public conveniences: See map
Public transport: Numerous city bus services

A meandering walk through the dark and atmospheric courts and closes of the Old Town; passing the grand Kirk of St Giles', Parliament House, the City Chambers and John Knox's House.

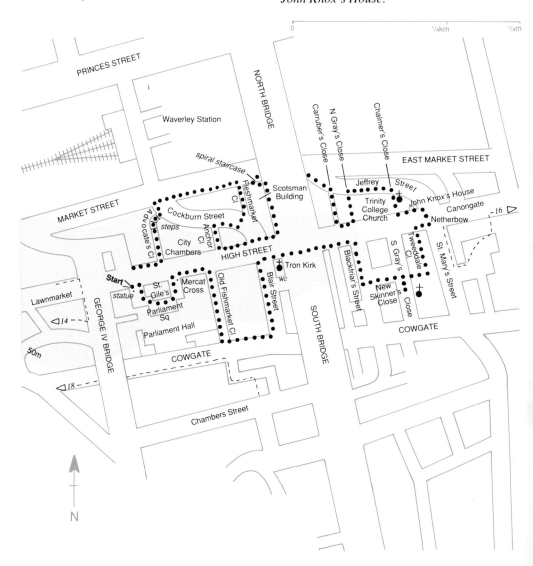

Start walking from the west end of Parliament Sq (see p. i), with the Lothian Region Offices (1900-5) to the right and the historic Kirk of St. Giles (earliest work from 15th century, but many subsequent additions and alterations) ahead. Walk down the roadside, leaving the statue of the 5th Duke of Buccleuch to the right, to the heart shape set into the cobbles – the site of the entrance to the Old Tolbooth jail. Turn right, across the entrance to the church, then turn left, behind it, with the building housing Parliament Hall and the High Court to the right (built in the 1630s, but remodelled in the Classical style by Robert Reid in the early 19th century), and passing the equestrian statue of Charles II (1685). Turn left at the end of the church, then right at the Mercat Cross (largely a 19th-century copy of the 15th-century original), down the right-hand side of the High St, with the City Chambers, fronted by its arched screen, on the far side of the road (built as the Royal Exchange; 1753-61).

After a short distance, turn right, down Old Fishmarket Cl. At the foot of the close turn left, along the dark and dingy Cowgate (p. iv). Just before the road passes beneath the South Bridge, climb left, up Blair St. At the top of the street, turn right, across the front of the Tron Kirk (John Mylne, 1633; steeple 1829, after the original was destroyed by fire).

Cross the end of South Bridge and continue down the High St beyond, before turning right, down Blackfriar's St. Halfway down turn left into New Skinner's Cl. Note the early 18th-century buildings to the right, and the fine modern housing to the left.

Turn right down South Gray's Cl for a short distance to St. Patrick's Church (1771, with later additions), then double back and turn right through the close to reach Tweeddale Cl. Cut left up the close, through its narrow entrance and back to the High St, then turn right.

Continue down the High St to the junction with St. Mary's St. St. Mary's St and Jeffrey St follow the line of the old city walls (p. iii), and this junction was the site of the Netherbow Port – one of the six city gates – beyond which was the separate burgh of Canongate. The port was built in 1513 and demolished in 1764, and insets in the road mark out the supposed positions of the two flanking towers. They also mark the end of the High St, so cross over and turn back up the far side.

After a short distance John Knox's House (16th century) is passed, with its external stairs and wooden frontages, jutting out into the High St. This is an interesting example of the type of building which once lined much of the street.

Continue a short distance beyond, then turn right, down Chalmer's Cl. On the right-hand side of the close is a building which now houses a brass rubbing centre, but which is, in fact, the remains of Trinity College Church (15th century); one of Scotland's finest mediaeval churches. The church was originally situated a short distance to the north, but it was demolished to clear the way for the extension to Waverley Station. Its stones were numbered, with the intention of re-building the church elsewhere, but, during the long period of argument over what should be done and by whom, most of the stones disappeared, and it proved impossible to build more than this small section; now hidden away down this dark close.

At the bottom of the close turn left, along Jeffrey St, then left again, up North Gray's Cl, to the High St. Turn right at the top for a short distance, then right again, down Carruber's Cl (Allan Ramsay opened a theatre here in 1736), back down to Jeffrey St.

Turn left, under the North Bridge, and then left again into the entrance to a spiral staircase which leads up to the Scotsman Building, the home of one of Scotland's national newspapers. Walk along the terrace to North Bridge, then turn right to return to the High St.

Turn right, across the top of Cockburn St, and continue, until Anchor Cl – where the Edinburgh edition of Burns' poems was published in 1787 – cuts down to the right.

At the foot of the narrow close, turn right up Cockburn St, then left, down narrow Fleshmarket Cl. At the foot of the close turn left, along Market St, then left again, up Cockburn St. After a short distance turn right, to climb up the steps of Advocate's Cl, leading back to the High St and St. Giles'.

16 Canongate

Length: 1 mile (1.5km)
Height climbed: Negligible
Grade: C
Public conveniences: See map
Public transport: Numerous city bus services

A walk along the eastern end of the Royal Mile, and through the closes to either side; passing Huntly House (City Museum), the Palace of Holyroodhouse (the royal residence in Edinburgh) and the Canongate Kirk.

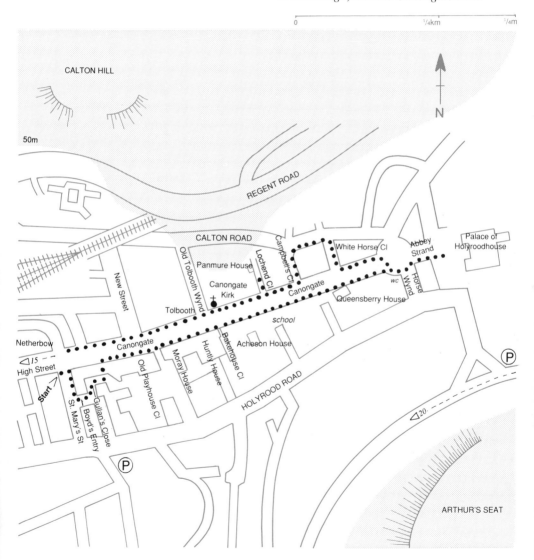

Start at the junction of St. Mary's St and the High St *(see p. i)*, on the site of the old Netherbow Port (built 1513, demolished 1764; metal plates in the road show the positions of the two flanking towers). This was one of the six gates in the old city walls *(p. iii)*, and beyond it lay the separate burgh of Canongate – named after the Augustinian canons of Holyrood, who were permitted by David I to build by the side of the road from Edinburgh to Holyrood.

Cross the top of St. Mary's St, then walk down its left-hand side. Midway down, turn left into Boyd's Entry. Veer left in the close, along Gullan's Cl, then right, around the central buildings, noting the fine 18th-century buildings to the right. Walk to the far left-hand corner of the close and cut through the close entry to join the Canongate.

Continue down the right-hand side of the road, noting the entrance to Old Playhouse Cl to the right (a theatre was opened in the close in 1747). A little beyond this are two fine examples of the type of houses which the Scottish nobility built for themselves in Edinburgh when it was still the country's centre of government: Moray House (early 17th century; easily recognised by its elongated pyramidic gate-posts) and Huntly House (1570). The former is now part of the Moray House College of Education, while the latter houses the City Museum, and contains many fascinating relics of Edinburgh's past, including the National Covenant of 1638 *(p. iv)*.

In the middle of the facade of Huntly House is the entrance to Bakehouse Cl – one of the best preserved of the Edinburgh closes – and just beyond is Acheson House (1633-34; now the Scottish Craft Centre).

Continue down the right-hand side of the Canongate, passing Queensberry House (1682, but much altered), towards the Palace of Holyroodhouse, at the foot of the Royal Mile.

The palace originated as a guest house for visitors to Holyrood Abbey (largely 13th-century, now ruined), but gradually grew in importance. The oldest remaining section is the north tower (to the left as you look at the front of the building) which was built in the 16th century for James IV. The rest of the building was built in the late 17th century, to a design by Sir William Bruce. The new design inluded a second tower, mirroring the old one.

From the palace, return to the Canongate, and start walking up its right-hand side. Turn right into White Horse Cl (the entrance is under a modern arcade). This charming court is another happy survival from the Old Town's heyday. It derived its name from the White Horse Inn (early 17th century; the building to the back of the court, facing the entrance); at one time an important coaching inn. Walk through the close and leave it by the exit to the left of the old inn; leading down to Calton Rd.

Turn left for a short distance, then left again, up Campbell's Cl, to the Canongate. Turn right for a short way, then right again, down Lochend Cl. At the foot of the close there is a large, plain, L-shaped mansion house. This is Panmure House (17th century); the home, from 1778-90, of the great economist Adam Smith, author of *The Wealth of Nations*.

Retrace your steps and continue up the Canongate to the Canongate Kirk (1688), with its curious curved gable. The churchyard contains the remains of a number of notable Edinburgh worthies. In the near-left corner lies Adam Smith (1723-90); while to the left of the church, in line with the far end of the building, is the grave of Robert Fergusson (1750-1774) *(p. viii)*: the poet laureate of the Old Town, whose vernacular poetry inspired Burns. Fergusson died young, poor and insane, and his grave remained unmarked until Burns provided a stone for it, during his first visit to the capital. Almost level with this, but set against the wall on the opposite side of the churchyard, is the grave of Mrs Maclehose: the 'Clarinda' of Burns' 'Sylvester and Clarinda' love letters. A blank stone up against the side of the church is thought to mark the grave of Rizzio, the murdered courtier of Mary Queen of Scots.

Continue up the Canongate, passing the old Canongate Tolbooth (1592; the old civic centre of this once independent burgh), with its clock and steeple, on the way back to the start of the route.

17 West Princes Street

Length: 1½ miles (2.5km)
Height climbed: Undulating
Grade: C
Public conveniences: See map
Public transport: Numerous city bus services

A walk leading from the Old Town to the New Town: starting in the Grassmarket and passing the Usher Hall, Princes St and West Princes St Gdns. Fine views of the castle.

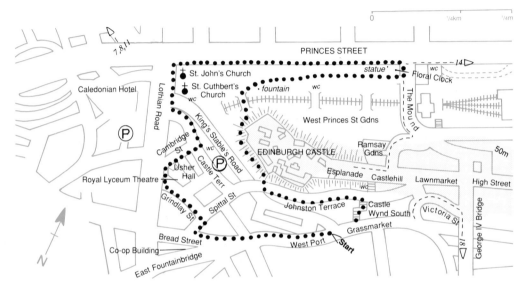

Start at the point where the West Port enters the Grassmarket *(see p. i)* – the site of the old west gate into the city. Walk along the West Port, noting the fine views of the castle between the buildings to the right.

When the road reaches a four-way junction bear half right, down Bread St – note the fine Co-op building on the corner ahead (1914) – then turn right, down Spittal St. Cross this and cut left, along Grindlay St. Follow this past the Royal Lyceum Theatre (1883) and the domed Usher Hall (1910), then walk round the front of the hall and continue along Cambridge St.

At the end of the street, cross Castle Terr and turn left. Follow the road until it joins Lothian Rd, then cut right, across the end of King's Stables Rd, and continue down Lothian Rd, noting the spire (1789) and towers (1894) of St. Cuthbert's Church in the trees to the right, and the huge Caledonian

Hotel (1898-1902) to the left.

Turn right beyond St. John's Church (1816-1879) along the right-hand side of Princes St; continuing until the Mound cuts up to the right. Turn into the Mound then right again, almost immediately, into West Princes St Gdns. Note the floral clock during the summer (first planted in 1904) and the statue of the poet Allan Ramsay, whose 18th-century octagonal house is incorporated into the white buildings of 19th-century Ramsay Gdns at the top of the slope to the left *(14)*.

Walk back through the gardens, bearing left after the fountain to reach a bridge over the railway. Across and a little beyond the bridge the track splits. Go left, and follow a clear path around the foot of the castle's basalt rock up to Johnston Terr. Continue up the right-hand side until the steps of Castle Wynd South drop down to the right, leading back to the Grassmarket.

18 Greyfriars

Length: 1¹/₂ miles (2.5km)
Height climbed: Undulating
Grade: C
Public conveniences: See map
Public transport: Numerous city bus services

A walk through the Old Town: starting in the Grassmarket and passing the National Library, the Cowgate, Greyfriars Church, Heriot's School and a section of the old city wall.

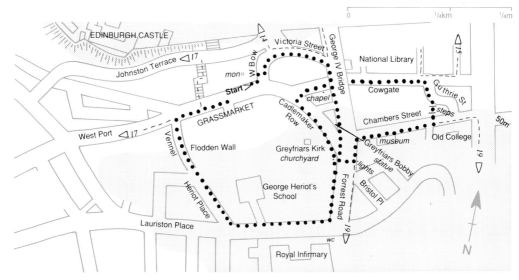

Start at the eastern end of the Grassmarket *(see p. i)*, near the monument to the Covenanters, and walk up the West Bow and the curving Victoria St beyond to join George IV Bridge. Notice the imposing National Library building (1956) opposite.

Cut right along George IV Bridge to the little statue of Greyfriars Bobby, the Skye terrier *(p. ii)*, then cross over (there is a crossing place at the far end of the road), and walk down Chambers St opposite. The right-hand side of the street is taken up by two buildings: the red-tiled 'Italian' palace which houses the Royal Scottish Museum (1861) and the neo-Classical Old College (Robert Adam, 1789). Cross Chambers St and turn left, down the steps leading to Guthrie St and, beyond that, the Cowgate. In 1771, Sir Walter Scott was born somewhere near the top of Guthrie St, in what was then called 'College Wynd'.

Turn left along the Cowgate, which runs under

George IV Bridge and, just beyond, passes the old tower of Magdalen Chapel (1621). At the junction beyond, turn left, up Candlemaker Row. Walk up the right-hand side of the road, and, as it approaches George IV Bridge, cut right into Greyfriars Churchyard. The church itself (dating, in part, from 1620) is rather undistinguished, but the churchyard is historically important as the place where the National Covenant was signed in 1638 *(p. iv)*, and the imposing monuments mark the graves of many famous Edinburgh figures *(p. ii)*.

Leave the cemetery and turn right, along Forrest Rd, then right again, along Lauriston Pl. On the right is the impressive mass of George Heriot's School (17th century). Beyond the school turn right, down Heriot Pl – passing a section of the Flodden Wall: the 16th-century town wall *(p. iii)* – then continue down the Vennel, back to the Grassmarket.

19 The Meadows

Length: 2 miles (3km)
Height climbed: Negligible
Grade: C
Public conveniences: See map
Public transport: Numerous city bus services

A walk through the Georgian and Victorian developments to the south of the Old Town; passing the Old College of the university and George Sq, and crossing the parkland of the Meadows.

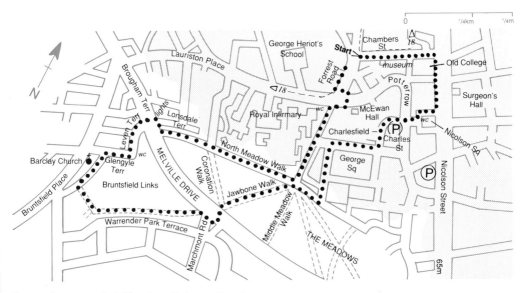

Start at the west end of Chambers St *(see p. i)* and walk down the right-hand side of the street. At the end of the street turn right, passing the entrance to the Old College (Robert Adam, 1789).

Carry on up the right-hand side of Nicolson St, then turn right into Nicolson Sq. Walk out of the far end of the square and across Potterrow, then continue beyond, noting the squat domed drum of McEwan Hall (completed 1897) ahead.

Turn left at the end of the car park and follow Charlesfield and Charles St into George Sq (now part of the university; 1763-4). Turn right, along the north side of the square, then left, down the west terrace. Sir Walter Scott lived at No 25 from 1774 to 1797.

Walk straight on, out of the square, to the edge of the parkland of the Meadows. Turn right to a junction of tracks and then half left, along tree-lined Jawbone Walk, across the Meadows to

Melville Drive. Cross this, then cut right across the foot of Marchmont Road and follow a broad path running inside the left-hand edge of Bruntsfield Links, parallel to the terraced houses of Warrender Park Terr. Turn right when a tarmac track heads off across the links, making straight for the tall steeple of Barclay Church (1864).

Turn right past the church, then right again, into Glengyle Terr, then left down Leven Terr. Cross Brougham Pl at the lights, to the left, then cross the end of Lonsdale Terr, and turn left along the path inside the edge of the Meadows, signposted for the City Centre.

When Jawbone Walk comes in from the right, turn left, up the tarmac walk between the university and the Royal Infirmary. At the top of the walk cross Lauriston Pl into Forrest Rd and then continue back to the start of the route.

(Warning: don't cross the parkland at night.)

20 Holyrood Park

Length: 4¹/₂ miles (7km)
Height climbed: 230ft (70m)
Grade: B
Public conveniences: See map
Public transport: Numerous city bus services

A steep walk through grassy hills to a small village; back by a disused railway. Fine views across the city.

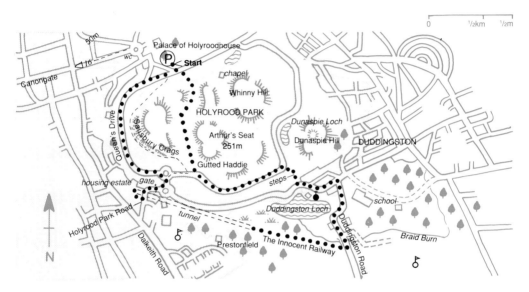

Start from the car park behind Holyroodhouse *(see p. i)*. Cross Queen's Drive and head half left up a path leading up and across the hillside. Follow this as it curves round a shoulder of the hill, and joins a clear tarmac road running up the right-hand side of a broad, grassy valley. After a short way, the tarmac finishes but a track continues, climbing up to a pass called the Gutted Haddie, under the shadow of Arthur's Seat.

Follow the track down to the road beyond the pass and turn left, for a little over half a mile (1km). After a short way, Duddingston Loch appears down to the right, and then, just as the road swings hard left, a path cuts off to the right, leading down to a high stone wall with trees beyond it. Walk down a flight of steps by the side of this wall, down to Duddingston – a small, semi-rural village, now surrounded by Edinburgh; famous chiefly for its church (12th century, with later additions) and

the Sheep's Heid Inn, thought to be the oldest licensed premises in Scotland.

After exploring the village, leave it along Duddingston Rd; walking on with the loch to the right. Just after the road crosses a very small burn, a path sets off to the right, signposted as the 'Innocent Railway'. This follows the route of one of Scotland's earliest railways (opened 1831), running between Edinburgh and Dalkeith.

After about a mile (1.5km) the line disappears into a well-lit tunnel, and then re-emerges in a housing estate. Carry straight on until a wall to the left ends; then turn left and double back to join Holyrood Park Rd. Turn left down this, through a gate and back into the park. A short distance beyond the gate there is a roundabout. To return to the start, either turn left, along the road, or climb up to the foot of Salisbury Crags, visible ahead, and turn left along a clear path.

21 Union Canal

Length: 2¹/₂ miles (4km)
Height climbed: Negligible
Grade: C
Public conveniences: See map
Public transport: Numerous city bus services

A walk along the towpath of an early industrial canal, and back through an area of attractive 19th-century housing.

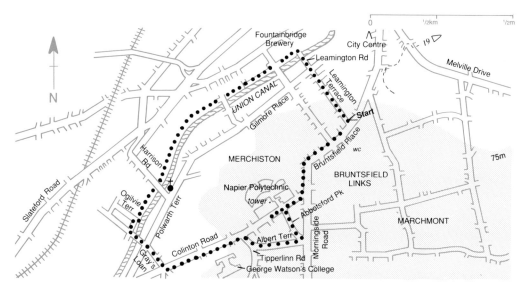

Start at the junction of Bruntsfield Pl and Leamington Terr, opposite the open parkland of Bruntsfield Links *(see p. i)*. Walk down Leamington Terr, with the Forth Estuary visible through the buildings ahead, to Gilmore Pl. Cross this and continue down Leamington Rd beyond to the canal.

The Union Canal was opened in 1822, as part of an inland water link between Glasgow and Edinburgh, but was closed in 1933, though some sections are now being reopened.

Cross over the canal, then turn left along the bank. At first this leads through the car park of Fountainbridge Brewery, but a clear path emerges beyond. Follow this for about a mile (1.5km), passing under three bridges (the third with a large church at its left end). Beyond the third, open parkland opens up to the right.

Just before the next bridge crosses the canal,

climb up to Ogilvie Terrace to the right, then cut left across the bridge. The route now runs through a pleasant residential area.

Cross Polwarth Terrace and continue up Gray's Loan, then turn left, down Colinton Rd. Continue along this, past George Watson's College, until Tipperlinn Road cuts off to the right. Turn down this, and then first left, along Albert Terrace (1863). As the road approaches Morningside Rd turn left, up Abbotsford Pk, back to Colinton Rd. On the far side of the road is Napier Polytechnic. Take a short detour to the left to see Merchiston Tower (15th century; the home of John Napier, who discovered logarithms) now forming the heart of the new polytechnic buildings.

Turn back, down Colinton Rd, and then left at the junction, down Morningside Rd and on along Bruntsfield Pl, back to the start of the route. (No link with *Walk 25*).

22 Colinton Dell

Length: 3 miles (5km)
Height climbed: Undulating
Grade: C
Public conveniences: Colinton
Public transport: Bus services between city centre and Slateford Rd

A series of clear paths through a picturesque wooded glen, leading to a small village within the suburbs of the city.

Colinton, on the south-western edge of the city, is one of those small villages which have been swallowed up by Edinburgh's expansion. The village is now a residential area, but in the past its inhabitants were largely dependent on the mills along the Water of Leith for their livelihood. The weirs in the wooded glen to the north of the village are all that remain of this industrial stage.

To reach this glen, drive south-west from the city centre along Dalry Rd and Slateford Rd (A70) for about three miles (5km). Just after bridges carrying the railway and the Union Canal cross the road, the Dell Inn appears to the left, at the start of the route. There is no car park, but it is possible to park in the side streets.

There are a number of paths beyond the inn. Keep to the clearest one, near the river. Follow this through mature woodland, past one bridge and then across a second. On the far side, turn hard left, along a clear path which rises up to join another, running parallel but above. Cross onto this upper path and continue; following the track through an old railway tunnel and then under a roadbridge beyond. Turn left immediately beyond the bridge, down a flight of steps to a footbridge across the river. Climb the steps beyond, leading up to the right of the bridge to Bridge Rd.

Cross the road and walk down Spylaw St beyond. At the bottom of the street veer left, across a road bridge, to the church (1771; remembered as a childhood haunt of Robert Louis Stevenson). Walk round to the left of the church, down Dell Rd, and follow the track beyond, through the woods by the turbulent Water of Leith.

Turn right across a wooden footbridge, then left by a mill lade. Follow this clear path until, just after a house, a track cuts off half left. Follow this down to a bridge across the river, then turn right, and follow the path back to the start.

23 Braid Hills

Length: 3¹/₂ miles (5.5km)
Height climbed: 500ft (150m)
Grade: C
Public conveniences: Hermitage of Braid
Public transport: Bus services between city centre
and Comiston Rd

*A good path through a wooded den, leading to
a short, steep hill climb and splendid views.*

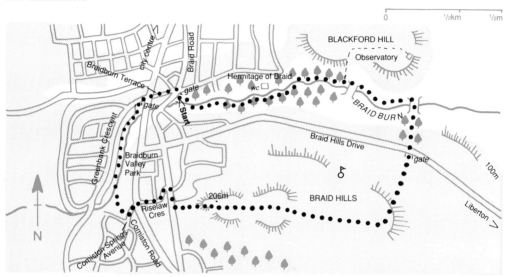

Just inside the southern edge of the city, the Braid
Hills rise to a modest 675ft (206m). Along the
northern edge of the hills runs a narrow, wooded
glen: the Hermitage of Braid.

The start of the walk is two and a half miles
(4km) south of the West End, and can be reached
by car along Lothian Rd, Bruntsfield Pl and
Morningside Rd. At the top of Morningside Rd,
head half left, up Braid Rd. Continue until a
footpath starts through a gate to the left, by the side
of the Braid Burn. Park by the road.

Follow the path for about a mile (1.5km);
passing through a steep-sided glen full of mature
woodland, and noting the Gothic mansion of
Hermitage of Braid (1785) in the heart of the glen.

When the wood ends, a bridge crosses the burn
to the right. Ignore this, and continue until a
second bridge appears. Cross this and climb the
path beyond, up a narrow line of trees between two

fields. Cross the road at the top of the path and go
through a gate onto the golf course beyond.

Climb straight up across the golf course
(making sure that no one is playing while you
cross) to a dyke. Turn right along a clear track
beside this, up to the highest point of the hill. The
view, given a decent day, is magnificent.

Follow the path beyond the summit down to
Braid Road. Cross it and turn right, then left, into
Riselaw Cr. When it ends, cross Comiston Rd and
continue down Comiston Springs Ave. After a
short distance, turn right into Braidburn Valley
Park and follow the paths through the open
parkland down to the gate at the far end of the park.
Turn right along Greenbank Cr, then cross
Comiston Rd once again and continue along
Braidburn Terr. Turn right down Braid Road to
return to the start.

24 Corstorphine Hill

Length: 3¹/₂ miles (5.5km)
Height climbed: 330ft (100m)
Grade: C
Public conveniences: Corstorphine
Public transport: Bus services between city centre
and Corstorphine

*A sequence of good footpaths across a low,
wooded hill, giving fine views over the city.*

Corstorphine Hill is a low, tree-covered ridge in the
west of the city; a clear landmark visible from
many of the walks in this book. There are many
paths running through the woods.

For this walk, start from Corstorphine: at one
time a separate village, but now little more than a
main street in the Edinburgh suburbs. It lies a little
over three miles (5km) west of the west end of
Princes St along Corstorphine Rd, just beyond the
zoo. Its main feature is its church (15th-century).

Park in one of the side streets and walk uphill
from St. John's Rd along Belgrave Terr and then
Clermiston Rd. Turn right into Old Kirk Rd and,
when it ends, turn left, up a clear path behind a row
of houses, leading to a small car park. Turn right,
through a gate onto the wooded hill. The path is
clear at first, then reaches a four-way junction.
Turn left, and start to climb uphill towards a tall
aerial on the peak of the hill, a little beyond which
is a Gothic tower: a memorial to Sir Walter Scott.

There are numerous paths through the woods at
this point. Try and find one which runs along the
ridge of the hill beyond the tower. It is difficult to
be certain of the exact route here, but there is no
real problem. Keep above the open fields down to
the left and you won't go far wrong.

When a clear track comes into view to the right,
join it. This runs along the right-hand edge of the
ridge, passing to the right of a fenced-off quarry,
and then dropping down towards Queensferry Rd.
Shortly before it reaches the road, a clear track
doubles back to the right, with a row of houses
beyond it. Follow this – along the bottom of the
wood, then climbing up to join another clear track.
Turn left along this, and follow it down to the edge
of a golf course. The path now becomes rough;
climbing, beside a fence, to join the perimeter fence
of Edinburgh Zoo. Turn right, along the fence, back
to the junction passed earlier and on to Corstorphine.

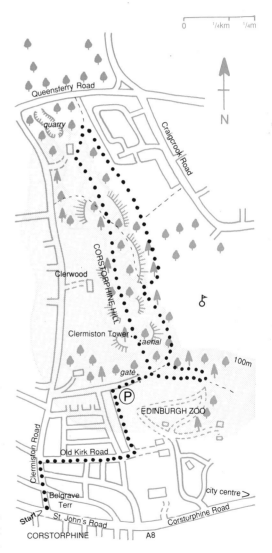

Walk 24

25 *Union Canal to Ratho*

Length: 6¹/₂ (10.5km) miles there and back
Height climbed: Negligible
Grade: B
Public conveniences: None
Public transport: Bus service between city centre
and Calder Road

A lineal walk along a canal towpath, through pleasant farmland, with a possible detour to a fine garden (open to the public), and an alternative return along public roads.

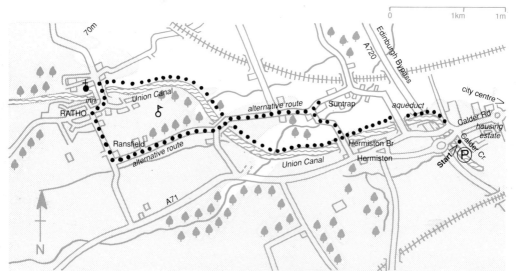

This route starts from the very edge of Edinburgh, five miles (8km) west of the west end of Princes St along Gorgie Rd and Calder Rd (the A71). Just before the road crosses the city bypass there is a signpost for the Union Canal, pointing left down Calder Cr. Follow this road for a short distance, into a housing estate, and then park in the public car park to the right.

Walk down to the canal and turn right, along the towpath. The Union Canal was opened in 1822, as part of the inland waterway link between Edinburgh and Glasgow (along with the Forth and Clyde Canal, completed in 1790, which it joins near Falkirk). It was closed to commercial traffic in 1933, but stretches are now navigable again.

The canal starts off northwards, under two road bridges, but then turns to the west and crosses the bypass on a dramatic aqueduct. Shortly beyond, the canal passes beneath a small road bridge with a

farm at one end of it. When the next road bridge (Hermiston Bridge) is reached, about a mile (1.5km) beyond the aqueduct, there is a possible diversion to Suntrap: a fine garden, owned by the National Trust for Scotland, about a mile (1.5km) north of the canal. To reach it, climb up to the road bridge and turn right; then right again at the next junction (there is a small fee on entry).

From Hermiston Bridge to Ratho by the canal is a further three miles (5km), through farmland and woodland, and there is an alternative route by road from Suntrap (see map) which is one mile (1.5km) longer. These roads can be quite busy during the summer, and there are no pavements, but visibility is generally good.

Ratho itself is a pleasant little village with a 16th-century church and a good inn, down by the canal side, from which boat trips operate up and down the canal. (No link with *Walk 21*.)

26 Roslin Glen

Length: 6 miles (9.5km)
Height climbed: Steep undulations
Grade: B
Public conveniences: Roslin
Public transport: Bus services between Edinburgh and Roslin

Out along rough paths through a wooded glen, passing a fine chapel and castle, and back along public roads and a disused railway line.

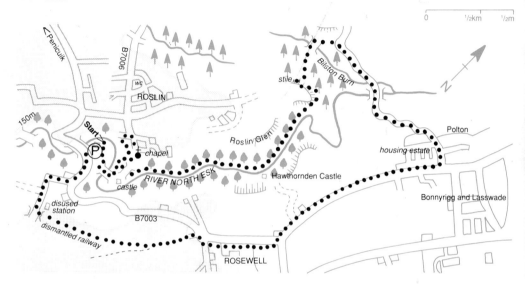

To reach the start of this walk, drive seven miles (11km) south of the city centre on the A701, then turn left on the B7006 to Roslin. Drive through the town then turn left down the road signposted to Roslin Glen. Follow this road into a steep valley. Just after crossing the river at the foot of the slope, turn left, into a large car park.

Follow the path from the far end of the car park, which leads to a footbridge over the River North Esk, then climbs and splits. A detour up the steps to the left leads to Rosslyn Chapel *(see p. xi)*.

Return to the split and take the other path; leading under the bridge which gives access to semi-ruinous Rosslyn Castle (oldest section 1304) and on to a footpath signposted for Polton. The path is vague at first, but becomes clearer as the glen deepens, and there is a fine view of Hawthornden Castle (17th century) *(p. vii)* on the far side of the glen.

Continue until the river doubles back to the right. At this point carry straight on, up to the top of a steep ridge, then turn left, and follow a path to a fence with a track on the far side of it. Cross the fence by a stile and turn right, then, a short distance beyond, left; down a track through conifers to a bridge over the Bilston Burn. Turn right on the far side of this to reach a small road.

Turn right along the road, to the bridge over the North Esk at Polton, then continue on the road; climbing up to join a larger road in a housing estate. Turn right and follow this for a mile (1.5km) to the edge of Rosewell, then cut right along a footpath signposted for Roslin. Just after crossing the B7003, the path splits. Take the right-hand track and follow it for a further mile (1.5km) to a disused station. Climb up onto the road bridge over the track and turn right, down to a junction. Turn left to return to the car park.

27 Boghall to Hillend

Length: 6 miles (9.5km)
Height climbed: 790ft (240m); undulating
Grade: B
Public conveniences: Hillend
Public transport: Bus service between city centre and Hillend

A steep hill circuit across farmland and moorland. Paths rough and views terrific.

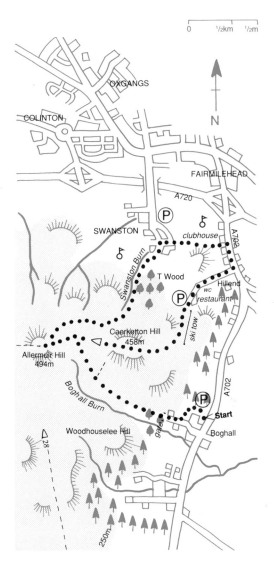

Start from the car park at Boghall *(see p. xiii)* and follow the fenced path which passes the farm buildings and joins a clear track. This leads up to the right of the wooded glen of the Boghall Burn.

Go through a gate level with a cottage and follow the track beyond, slowly rising through rough grazing land towards a small heathery corrie in the lee of Allermuir Hill.

A little over a mile (1.5km) after the start, the track enters a field. Walk up to the far right hand corner of the field and cross a stile, then immediately cut right across another stile. Beyond this, a path climbs straight up the slope ahead. Ignore this and follow a rough path which heads half left up and across the face of the hill; leading up to the nick in the skyline between Caerketton and Allermuir.

Turn left along the ridge towards Allermuir – noting the fine views across Edinburgh and the Forth below – before cutting back to the right on a clear, grassy path, running across the face of the hill towards the T Wood. Follow the path between the wood and the Swanston Burn down to the tiny, whitewashed village of Swanston, where Robert Louis Stevenson stayed as a boy.

Turn right from the village, along a straight track leading to the golf course club house, then right again, along the A702, to reach the end of the drive up to the Hillend ski-slopes. Walk up to the car park and restaurant, then continue, up the right-hand side of the slopes, and on to the peak of Caerketton. Turn right, along the ridge, to return to the point where the path up the Boghall Burn climbs up from the left.

28 Castlelaw to Dreghorn

Length: 3¹/₂ miles (5.5km) one way
Height climbed: 530ft (160m)
Grade: B
Public conveniences: None
Public transport: Bus services between city centre and both Colinton and Flotterstone

Steep, lineal hill-crossing through grazing land and moorland. Paths rough, but generally clear and views splendid. Reverse route clear. Possible return route by Walk 29.

Start from the car park at Castlelaw *(see p. xiii)*, and walk up the hill to the iron age Castlelaw Fort *(p. xi)*. The fort contains a well-preserved souterrain: a 76 ft (23m) tunnel, illuminated by modern skylights.

Walk up the clear track to the right of the fort enclosure, noting the army firing ranges in the depression down to the left. When the range is in use a red flag will be flown at the start of the route, in which case **do not stray to the left of the path**.

Ignore the track cutting off to the right, and continue climbing up and across the side of Castlelaw Hill. As the track draws level with the peak of the hill, to the left, another track leads off to the left, up to the summit. Ignore this and continue; climbing up to the low peak of Fala Knowe, where another path cuts off to the right. Ignore this once again and continue to a four-way junction. Carry straight on to a further junction, on the watershed between Allermuir Hill and Capelaw Hill. The path to the right leads up to the summit of Allermuir Hill, and then joins *Walk 27*. But for this route, drop straight down the valley of the Howden Burn on a clear track, noting the fine views ahead to the Firth of Forth.

The path crosses the burn at the Green Craig Cistern (dated 1790; part of an early city water supply), at which point the route becomes less clear. Head half left, across an area of rough grazing, to the nearest corner of a small wood. Turn left along the top of this wood, crossing a small burn, then turn right, through a gate, and follow the path beyond to the bottom of the wood.

For Dreghorn *(p. xii)*, carry straight on down the track ahead to join a metalled road and turn right. Alternatively, head half left across a field to join the footpath between Colinton and Bonaly *(p. xii)*; providing a possible link for a return to Castlelaw along *Walk 29*.

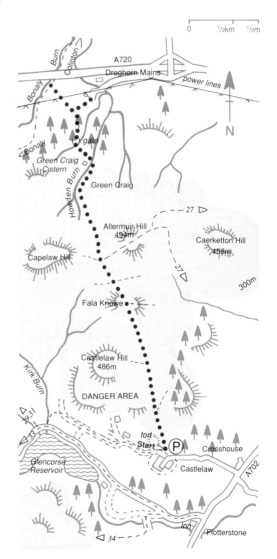

29 Bonaly to Castlelaw

Length: 4 miles (6.5km) one way
Height climbed: 550ft (170m); undulating
Grade: B
Public conveniences: Bonaly
Public transport: Bus services between city centre
and both Colinton and Flotterstone

*A walk through heather moorland and farm-
land; leading up to a low hill pass on paths of
varying quality. Reverse route clear. Possible return on Walks 31 and 30 or 28.*

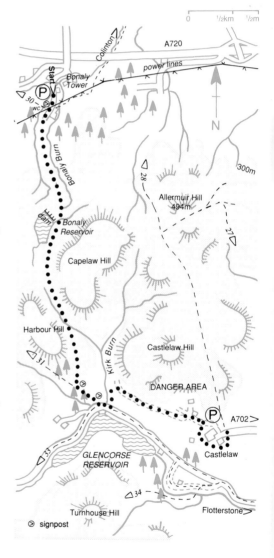

Start from the car park beyond Bonaly Tower *(see
p. xii)* and follow the clear track leading up the hill
beyond; out of the woodland, across a clear area,
then back into woodland again. At this point there
is a Right of Way signpost indicating the footpath
to Glencorse Reservoir. Follow the clear track
beyond, through the trees and on up the slope
beyond to Bonaly Reservoir.

Pass to the left of the reservoir and then
continue to climb – the path becoming less clear
now – up into the low pass between Harbour Hill
and Capelaw Hill. Drop down the rather damp
glen beyond. The rough path re-emerges to the left
of the burn, but quickly crosses it to the right, then
climbs over the end of Harbour Hill, leaving a
stand of conifers to the right, before dropping down
into the neighbouring glen, and reaching a Right of
Way signpost beside a stand of trees by the burn
side. Turn left by the trees, down to the road along
Glencorse Reservoir. There is a Right of Way
signpost for Colinton at the foot of the path.

Turn left along the road for a short distance,
until it crosses the Kirk Burn and turns to the right.
Just beyond the burn, turn left (there is no path) up
the slope, to join a clear track running across the
side of Castlelaw Hill. Turn right along this,
looking out for the red flags which indicate that the
army firing ranges (at the far end of the track) are
in use; in which case you should drop back down to
the tarmac road below and walk down to join the
A702 at Flotterstone *(Walk 31)*.

Otherwise, follow the track to Castlelaw Farm.
Walk round to the right of the buildings, through a
series of fields, then rejoin the clear road beyond
them; just opposite the entrance to the car park.

Walk straight up through the car park to reach
the start of *Walk 28*; otherwise turn right and
follow the metalled road for half a mile (1km) to
reach the A702.

Walk 29

30 Currie

Length: 4 miles (6.5km)
Height climbed: 400ft (120m)
Grade: B
Public conveniences: Currie; Juniper Green
Public transport: Bus service between city centre and Currie

A short circuit through wooded glens and open farmland, offering fine views across Edinburgh and the Forth. Paths of varying quality.

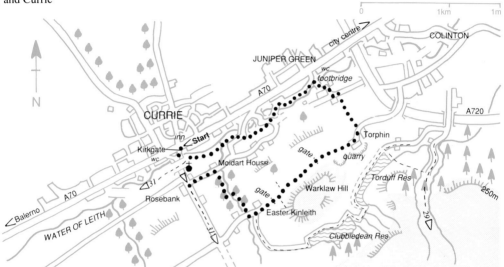

Park in the centre of Currie *(see p. xiii)* and turn down the road signposted for Currie Kirk (Kirkgate). Follow the road past the church and on to Rosebank Farm, then turn left along a straight public road between fields.

Just beyond Moidart House, to the left, cross a stile to the right of the road, and follow the path beyond, leading up a line of trees, with a high wall to the left. When the wall cuts across the line of the path, cross a stile, through the wall, and follow the path beyond. Cross a footbridge below a small pond, then carry on up the glen to the road.

Turn left, past Easter Kinleith Farm. At this point a track winds up to the right – the start of a three mile (5km) path to Bonaly via Clubbiedean and Torduff Reservoirs. For this route, however, carry straight on, through the farmyard and on up a track beyond, climbing gently between fields.

At the end of the fields there is a gate, beyond

which the main track swings right, while this route cuts left, on a rough footpath. After a short distance this path splits. This time go right, along the face of the hill.

After a short distance a fence cuts across the path with a gate in it, beyond which the track continues, much more clearly, down to Torphin Quarry and the junction with the road. Opposite the entrance to the quarry a path leads down to the left, between two fields. Follow this path down to a road and cut left. Just before the road reaches a farm, turn right and follow the road which zig-zags down to the Water of Leith, then crosses it by a footbridge. At the far side of the bridge turn left, along a clear path. Just beyond the building at Woodhall the path splits: keep left. Further on it splits again: this time take the right-hand path, and follow it until Currie Kirk appears to the left, and a flight of steps to the right, leading down to the Kirkgate.

31 Maiden's Cleuch

Length: 5 miles (8km) one way
Height climbed: 500ft (150m)
Grade: A/B
Public conveniences: Flotterstone; Currie
Public transport: Bus services between city centre and both Flotterstone and Currie

A gradual climb to a low hill pass on paths of varying quality. Reverse route clear. Possible loop including stretch by Water of Leith, and alternative return routes by Walks 30 and 29 or 32 and 33.

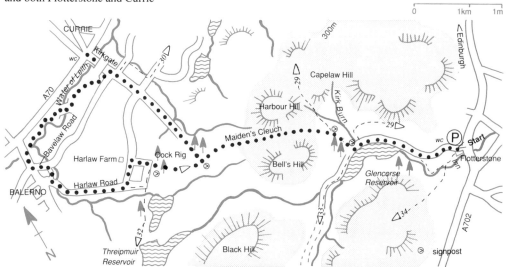

Start from the car park behind the Flotterstone Inn *(see p. xiii)* and walk up the tarmac road leading to Glencorse Reservoir. Walk up the eastern side of the reservoir until the Kirk Burn comes in from the right and the road turns to the left.

Just beyond the burn there is a gate to the right, and a Right of Way signpost for Currie and Balerno. Turn right up a rough path to the right of a wood. After a short distance a path cuts off to the right, leading to Colinton *(Walk 29)*. Ignore this, and carry on, along a clear path to a stile in the pass of Maiden's Cleuch, between Harbour Hill and Bell's Hill.

A little over a mile (1.5km) beyond the pass, across damp, heather moorland, the path reaches a stile in a dyke at Cock Rig. Beside this there is a Right of Way signpost, indicating a number of routes. Turn right, on the path to Currie, and follow a line of conifers down to a quiet public

road. Cross this and continue down the public road beyond – the Kirkgate – to reach Currie.

An alternative return of seven and a half miles (12km) can be made to Flotterstone via Balerno. Just after the Kirkgate passes the 18th-century church, the route of a disused railway crosses the road. Climb onto this, and follow the footpath which runs along it for about a mile and a half (2.5km), until it joins the road on the edge of Balerno. Turn left into the town then, after the road has crossed the Water of Leith, turn left again, up Bavelaw Rd; then left once more, up Harlaw Rd. Follow this road out of the town, and stay with it until it reaches Harlaw Farm, then turn right, up a broad track. At the end of this track, just beyond a plantation of conifers, carry straight on along the path signposted for Glencorse. This rejoins the original track at Cock Rig.

32 Threipmuir Reservoir

Length: 5 miles (8km)
Height climbed: None
Grade: C
Public conveniences: None
Public transport: Bus service between city centre and Balerno

A low-level circuit on good tracks through farmland and woodland, passing two reservoirs.

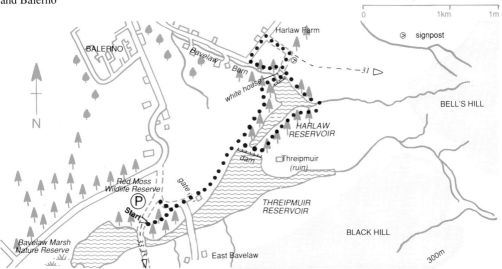

Start walking from the car park by Threipmuir Reservoir *(see p. xiii)* – a parking place for visitors to the Red Moss Wildlife Reserve and the Bavelaw Marsh Nature Reserve (see map). To the east of the road a wedge of trees comes in; walk along the path to the right of these. At the end of the trees it joins a good track and continues; through the fishermen's car park, past the end of the drive to East Bavelaw and through a gate, then on, between farmland and the reservoir, to the dam.

At the dam keep left, then continue along a good track through pine woodland by the side of Harlaw Reservoir. At the end of the reservoir follow the track to the right of a two-storey white house by the dam, then turn left along a tarmac road.

Follow this road until it bends sharply to the right. At this point carry straight on, down a rough path through the trees above the Bavelaw Burn, with fields to the right. Follow the path to its end, where it joins a narrow road. To the left at this junction it is a mile (1.5km) walk along the public road back to Balerno but, for this route, walk to the right, until Harlaw Farm is reached. Turn right, up a good track starting opposite the farm. Follow this to a junction at the edge of a conifer plantation. The path straight ahead is signposted as a footpath to Glencorse *(Walk 31)*, but for this route cut right, along the edge of the trees, back to the white house by Harlaw Reservoir.

Turn left along the end of the reservoir, then follow a clear path round the water, through pine woodland, back to the foot of Threipmuir. Turn right, across the dam, then left, back to the start along the original track.

33 Bavelaw to Flotterstone

Length: 6 miles (9.5km) one way
Height climbed: 100ft (30m)
Grade: B
Public conveniences: Flotterstone
Public transport: Bus services between city centre and both Balerno and Flotterstone

A low-level, lineal route on good tracks; leading through a narrow glen and past two reservoirs. Possible return routes by Walks 31 and 32 or Walks 34 and 35. Reverse route clear.

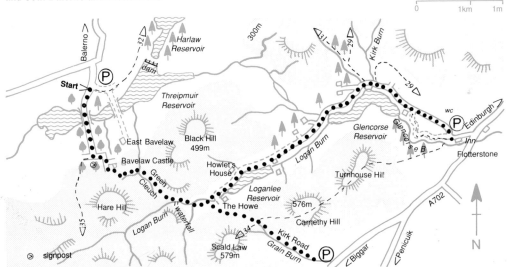

Start from the car park by Threipmuir Reservoir *(see p. xiii)* and walk south, across the bridge over the reservoir and then up the beech-lined avenue beyond. At the junction at the top of the avenue there is a Right of Way signpost, indicating paths to Nine Mile Burn *(Walk 35)*, to the right, and Flotterstone, to the left.

Turn left and follow the road past the entrance to Bavelaw Castle (mainly 17th century) and on to the end of the woodland. Cross a stile and cut half left across grazing land, following a faint path marked by posts. After a short distance the path drops down to cross a small burn, beyond which it is much clearer; winding towards the entrance of Green Cleuch. Follow the path through the cleuch: a narrow glen of scree and heather. Near the far end of the glen, the Logan Burn enters from the right, down a fine waterfall

Follow the widening glen round to The Howe –

a house at the near end of Loganlee Reservoir. Just before the house, a path cuts up to the right, to the hill pass between Scald Law (the highest point in the Pentlands) and Carnethy Hill. This is the Kirk Road (the old road to Penicuik Church), and leads down, by the Grain Burn, to a car park by the A702 *(p. xiii)*; a distance of just under two miles (3km).

For this walk, ignore this path and carry straight on, along the edge of Loganlee Reservoir (noting the 16th-century ruin of Howlet's House by a burn to the left), then on down the glen to Glencorse Reservoir. Near the point where the Kirk Burn flows in to the reservoir, *Walks 29* and *31* set off up the hills to the left; while under the water in this corner of the reservoir are the sunken ruins of the 13th-century St Catherine's Chapel *(p. xi)*.

Follow the tarmac track along the waterside and beyond, down to Flotterstone.

34 Five Peaks

Length: 7 miles (11km) one way
Height climbed: 1000ft (300m); steep undulations
Grade: A
Public conveniences: Flotterstone
Public transport: Bus services between city centre and both Flotterstone and Balerno

A steeply undulating walk across five peaks. Views magnificent; paths rough but clear and generally dry. Possible return route by Walk 33. **Pointers to reverse route in italics.**

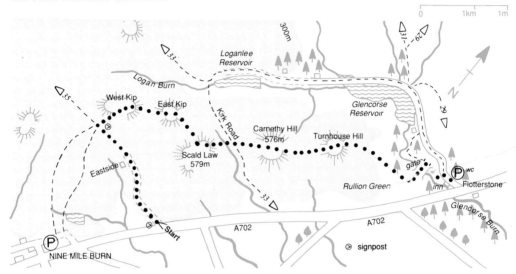

Start from either Nine Mile Burn or the Right of Way signpost a mile and a half (2.5km) to the east, along the A702, at the foot of the Eastside path *(see p. xiii)*. The route from Nine Mile Burn to the pass at the head of Eastside Glen is described in *Walk 35*. For the Eastside path, climb up a clear, dry track, through grazing land, leading up to the right of Eastside Farm, and on up to the pass beyond.

Once at the highest point of the path, turn right and follow a rough path which climbs up to the conical peak of West Kip.

The route is not in any doubt; running over the five peaks of West Kip, East Kip, Scald Law – at 1899ft (579m) the highest point in the Pentlands – Carnethy Hill and Turnhouse Hill. The steep sides of these volcanic hills make for strenuous walking, but the path is generally clear, and the views in all directions are spectacular.

Between Scald Law and Carnethy Hill the route

crosses the Kirk Road path *(Walk 33)* between the A702, to the right, and the valley of the Logan Burn to the left. If the weather becomes bad then the track along the Logan Burn offers a low-level alternative route to Flotterstone.

From the peak of Turnhouse Hill, the path heads half-right, down a ridge with scattered trees on it. To the right at this point is the site of the battle of Rullion Green (1666) *(p. xii)*. Follow this ridge until it ends near the Glencorse Burn. Cross a footbridge over the burn, go through a gate and turn right for a short distance to reach the tarmac road. Turn right along this to reach Flotterstone; left to reach *Walks 29, 31* and *33*.

If walking this route in reverse, start from the car park behind the Flotterstone Inn (p. xiii) and walk on along the tarmac road until a path cuts left, along the riverside. After crossing the burn the route is quite clear.

35 Kitchen Moss

Length: 5 miles (8km) one way
Height climbed: 600ft (180m)
Grade: B
Public conveniences: None
Public transport: Bus services between city centre and Balerno

A short, low hill crossing through farmland and moorland. Paths clear and good. Possible return route by Walk 36, or by using paths from Walks 33 and 34. Reverse route clear.

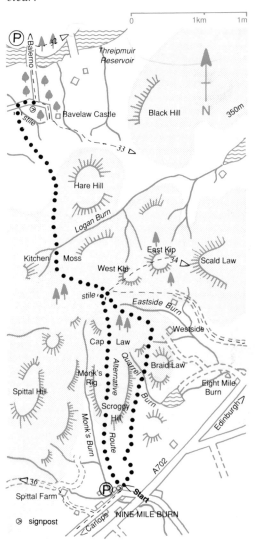

Start from the hamlet of Nine Mile Burn *(see p. xiii)* and walk through the gate at the northern end of the houses, marked by a Right of Way signpost for Balerno. Walk on beyond the gate through two fields, then turn left and climb up the hill with a dyke to the left. Cross the dyke at the top of the field, then turn half right along a faint path leading into the valley of the Quarrel Burn. The path is marked by posts and its route is quite clear, leading up to a dip between two rounded hills, through which the pointed peak of West Kip is visible.

From the dip, cut left along a rough path above Westside Farm and below a stand of conifers. The path leads around the head of the glen to the pass below West Kip. (There is an alternative route from Nine Mile Burn to this pass. Turn left through the gate and climb up the ridge of Scroggy Hill and on across Monks Rig and Cap Law – see map. The route is less clear this way.)

There is a fence running up through the pass. Cross the stile over this and join a track running along the far side of the fence. This track has run up the east side of the glen, from the A702, and is another alternative start to this walk (see map).

Turn left along the track, which drops gently down into the broad moorland swale of Kitchen Moss. The route is quite clear, leading first towards a small conifer plantation, then turning right, crossing the Logan Burn on a stone bridge, and climbing onto the ridge on the far side of the moss. Go through a gate in a dyke and drop down the far side of the ridge, following a track by a dyke down to the woods around the private Bavelaw Castle (mainly 17th century). Carry straight on until the path crosses a stile and runs through a narrow wood to join a clear track. Turn right along this to a junction. To the left from the junction it is two and a half miles (4km) to Balerno. Alternatively, carry straight on to reach *Walk 33*.

Walk 35

36 The Bore Stane

Length: 6 miles (9.5km) to Buteland
Height climbed: 430ft (130m)
Grade: A
Public conveniences: None
Public transport: Bus services between city centre and both Carlops and Balerno

A fine walk across a hill pass on rough, clear tracks. Possible return by by routes 35 or 37. Reverse route clear.

There are two possible paths from Carlops *(see p. xiii)* along which to start this route. From the southern end of the little village a metalled track leads up to the west of the valley of the North Esk, but this is the duller of the two paths. The other starts at the northern end of Carlops, just by the bridge, and is signposted for Kirknewton.

Turn off the road onto this path, which starts in a wooded den, then continues up a narrow, grassy glen. After half a mile (1km) a footbridge crosses the river. Cross this and climb up the slope beyond to join the metalled track from Carlops; leading up past Fairliehope Farm and on towards the North Esk Reservoir.

Just as the track starts to turn down towards a cottage by the reservoir, a signpost indicates that a Right of Way heads off to the left. If the track by the cottage is followed, it leads over a low pass and drops down by Spittal Farm to join a track between Carlops and Nine Mile Burn (see map). For the Bore Stane, however, cross a stile beyond the Right of Way signpost, leading in to a field. Cross this field, and the burn at its far end, and climb up to walk around the right-hand edge of a conifer plantation; then drop down to the reservoir, and walk on beside a fence up the valley of the Henshaw Burn. After a short way there is a gate in the fence. Go through this, then over a footbridge, and continue up the right-hand side of the glen; up to a heathery pass, where there are some conifers, and, beside them, the rocky outcrop of the Bore Stane.

Follow the path on, down into the valley of the Bavelaw Burn and on to join the drive which leads from Listonshiels to the left. Beyond this there is a junction, with a footpath cutting right to Balerno – three miles (5km) – and a straight driveway leading down to the public road at Buteland. Turn right along this public road for around three miles (5km) to reach Balerno.

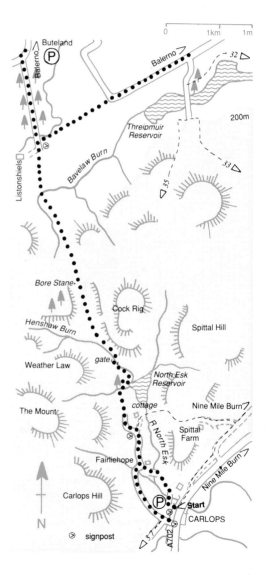

Walk 36

37 Cauldstaneslap

Length: 7¹/₂-8 miles (12-13km) one way
Height climbed: 530ft (160m)
Grade: A
Public conveniences: West Linton
Public transport: Bus service between city centre and West Linton

A fine lineal walk through a high hill pass. Paths clear at the southern end, but damp and vague about Harperrig. Possible return route by Walk 36. **Pointers for reverse route shown in italics.**

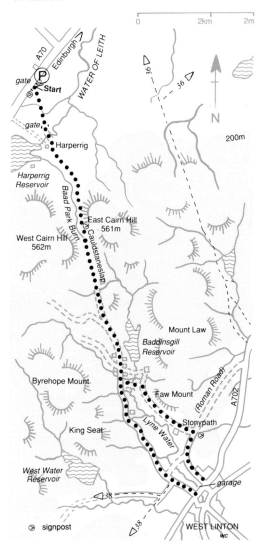

The northern end of this track is in the bleak grazing land around the head of the Water of Leith *(see p. xiii)*. Look for the signpost for the footpath to West Linton and go through a gate from the road. There is no path beyond; just walk on keeping a dyke to the left. At the end of the dyke (latterly only a pile of stones) go through a gate, then cross a footbridge over the Water of Leith. Climb the bank beyond, go through a kissing gate, and continue with a fence to the right. The route at this point, through fields, is difficult to discribe, but is well marked with yellow arrows.

Beyond the fields the path is clear; climbing the steep slope to the left of the Baad Park Burn towards the col between East Cairn and West Cairn Hills: Cauldstaneslap. In the pass itself there is a fence, a stile, and a Right of Way signpost. Carry straight on, along a clear path through rough moorland; dropping down gently, past Baddinsgill Reservoir and the cluster of houses below it.

A little beyond the last of these houses, a path drops down towards a bridge across the Lyne Water. At this junction there is a choice of routes.

The quickest route is straight on down the tarmac road to West Linton; but the more pleasant walking is on the far side of the glen, though this adds half a mile (1km) to the route. Cross the bridge, then follow a built up path beyond, around the end of a field. Climb onto the steep face of Faw Mount and turn right, down a clear path which leads down the glen to Stonypath Farm. A little beyond this there is a junction and a signpost. Turn right – a turn to the left leads two miles (3km) to Carlops, and a link with *Walk 36* – then follow this new track until another track branches off to the left. Follow this down to West Linton.

The reverse of this route is easily followed, starting up the road beside the Gordon Arms Garage in West Linton.

38 West Linton to Garvald

Length: 8 miles (13km)
Height climbed: 260ft (80m) undulating
Grade: A
Public conveniences: West Linton
Public transport: Bus service between city centre and West Linton

Pleasant circular route through farmland and woodland. There is a possible alternative route to the north; 2 miles (3km) longer (see map). Some navigation is required for this extension.

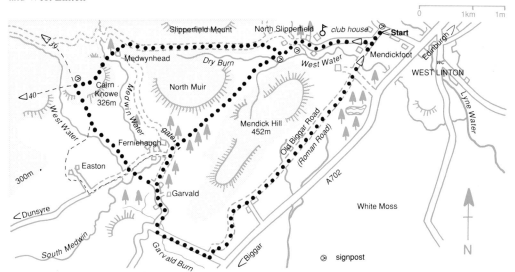

Walk along the golf club road, above West Linton *(see p. xii).* Ignore the first sign for Dunsyre and continue to the house at Mendickfoot, where a path cuts off to the left – the Old Biggar Road to Dolphinton. Ignore this and follow the main tarmac road; past North Slipperfield and across the West Water. Just after the burn, cut left at the signpost for Boston Cottage, along a clear track.

After a short distance there is another signpost. Carry straight on along a clear, grassy track. Follow this down a valley, through rough grazing land, and latterly to the right of a plantation of conifers. Go through the gate at the end of the trees, past the house at Ferniehaugh and down the drive beyond. When the drive reaches a junction, go left, down to Garvald Farm.

Follow the road beyond the farm. When it reaches a T junction (just after crossing the Garvald Burn), go left. Continue along this minor

road until, just before it reaches the A702, a track cuts off to the left, signposted for 'Sandy Nick'. Turn onto this and follow it, through farmland and woodland, back to Mendickfoot.

The track by Medwynhead is more exposed and longer. To follow it, turn uphill from the signpost on Slipperfield Mount (see map) to join a clear track. Follow this for 1$\frac{1}{2}$ miles (2.5km), until a small plantation appears, across the moorland to the left. Walk past this (the cottage of Medwynhead is sheltered beyond it), across the Medwin Water beyond, and up on to the low hill of Cairn Knowe. Find the signpost on the far side of the hill and turn left, down to the West Water (for a full description of this section of the route, see *Walk 39*). Follow the burn down to a track, and turn left for a short distance to reach Ferniehaugh.

A large-scale map is recommended for this northerly route *(p. xiii).*

39 Covenanter's Grave

Length: 6 miles (9.5) one way
Height climbed: 600ft (180m)
Grade: A
Public conveniences: None
Public transport: None

A tough route following an unclear track across rough, boggy moorland and grazing land. Possible loop, return by Walk 40, or link with Walk 38. **Pointers for reverse route in italics.**

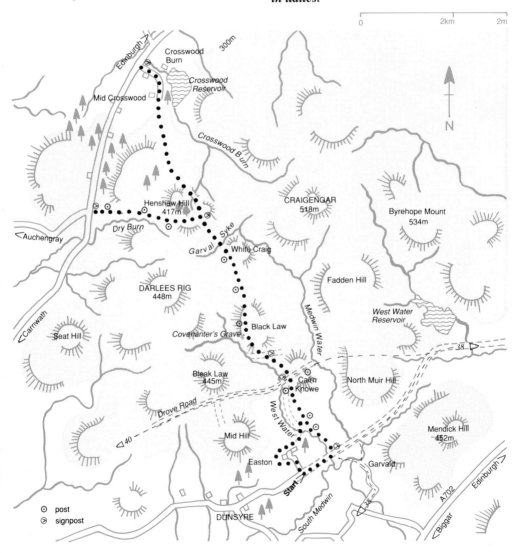

From the foot of the Easton Farm drive *(see p. xii)*, continue along the line of the road and cross the West Water on a footbridge by a ford. A short distance beyond, there is a Right of Way signpost for Crosswood, pointing to the left. Walk up the right-hand side of the burn for about half a mile (1km) until a post is reached, then, as the burn swings left, walk across the moor towards another post.

At this post a path joins from the left. To return to the start, follow this across the West Water, round the right-hand edge of a plantation, and down past Easton Farm to the road.

Otherwise, walk on across the damp, rising moorland. There is no clear path, but the low mound of Cairn Knowe is visible at the end of the slow rise. A post is visible on the right of the hill. Ignore this, and head to the left of the peak. As you approach, a post appears below the horizon to the left. Walk past this and continue to a metal Right of Way signpost on the ridge beyond, indicating the routes for West Linton *(Walk 38)*, Dolphinton (back the way), Boston Cottage *(Walk 40)* and Crosswood. *Looking back (for those walking the path in reverse), the wood behind Easton is visible; with the path running up to it from the West Water. Head towards the point where this path joins the West Water. When the post by the burn becomes visible, cut left down the burn.*

Looking ahead, there is a track running across the slope of Black Law, and a faint path heading towards it. Follow this, making for a Right of Way signpost by the side of the track. *Looking back from this post, the post on Cairn Knowe is visible.*

Walk straight across the track and start climbing up the slope beyond, leaving the highest point of the hill to the right. A little to the left of the summit is the Covenanter's Grave *(p. xii)*, and a short distance beyond that is a post, beyond which a faint path leads off across the moor, with the low ridge of Darlees Rig to the left. There is a second post at the lowest part of the path, and a third is visible where it climbs up to the left of White Craig. *Looking back from this third post, the route is clear in the reverse direction.*

Ahead is Henshaw Hill, with two stunted rowan trees on its peak. Drop down and cross Garval Syke, then climb up to a Right of Way signpost, visible on the horizon. This indicates paths to Dunsyre and West Linton (back the way), Harburn and Auchengray. *Looking back, the last post, to the right of White Craig, is visible.*

From the signpost, there are two alternative routes down to the road, of which the Auchengray route is the simpler. For this, cut left, along the face of Henshaw Hill, gradually curving to the right, until a post is reached, from where the A70 is visible ahead. Continue on the dry ground up to the right of the Dry Burn; through a gate, past two posts, then on to a fence with a gate in it. Turn right along this to the Right of Way signpost (Dolphinton and West Linton) by the road. *Looking back, the last post is visible, and the route clear, up the burn and then to the right of Henshaw Hill.*

It is possible to make a loop of this route by turning right along the A70 for two miles (3km) to Crosswood, where, at the end of a drive, there is a signpost for Dolphinton. Walk along the drive until a conifer plantation comes in from the right. Turn right along the edge of the trees. At the end of the plantation, cross a stile and head half left across a field to another stile. Cross this and follow a clear track across a field. When the track turns right, carry straight on, to a further stile. Cross this and continue; walking through rough grazing, with a field to the left. When a fence crosses the way, look for the gate in it, then head half right beyond, up to the far corner of a field. Leave the field by a gate, and walk on to the left of the dyke beyond.

Just as the dyke approaches a small valley it is crossed by a stile. Climb to the top of this and look ahead, noting the two rowans on the top of Henshaw Hill. Beyond the stile, cross a footbridge over the burn and then walk on, heading to the left of the trees. A short distance beyond them, there is a dyke with a gate in it. Go through this and continue to the post at the junction of the paths, visible ahead.

If you are walking this complicated path in the reverse direction, look for Crosswood Reservoir in the distance, and the plantation to its left, and use these to help navigation.

A large-scale map is recommended for this route. *(p. xiii)*

40 Boston Cottage to Dunsyre

Length: 5 miles (8km) one way
Height climbed: 260ft (80m)
Grade: A
Public conveniences: None
Public transport: None

A low hill-crossing on open moorland, with paths rough and uncertain in places. There is a possible return by Walk 39. **Pointers for reverse route in italics.**

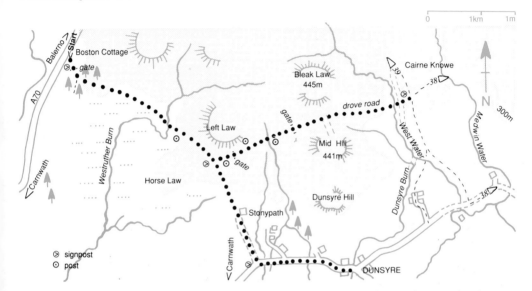

Boston Cottage *(see p. xiii)* no longer exists, except as a loose pile of stones to the west of the A70, opposite a small conifer plantation, but the path starts clearly enough.

Go through a gate, marked by a signpost for Dunsyre, and walk across a small field towards the trees. Pass through a gate in a fence and follow the track beyond through the plantation. When this splits, take the left hand path and follow it to the edge of the trees.

Beyond the plantation is a broad, heathery moor, with a faint path running across it. After a mile (1.5km) the path is crossed by the Westruther Burn (sizable when in spate, and no bridge), and a little beyond is a post. *Looking back from this point the route is quite clear: heading towards a gap in the conifers from which the path emerges.*

Continue on this path for just under a mile (1.5km) to a signpost, indicating paths to West

Linton, Dunsyre and Boston Cottage. Another post is visible to the left, but ignore this and carry straight on along the path to Dunsyre. The way is clear: down through a gate and on, to the right of the buildings at Stonypath. Turn left, through a gate, at the end of the buildings, then right, through the main gate, and on down the drive to the road. Turn left along the road to reach Dunsyre. *There is a sign at the foot of the drive for Boston Cottage, and the reverse route is quite clear.*

The connecting path between this route and *Walk 39* is less clear. From the signpost on Left Law (see map) follow three more posts (the third by a small burn), then climb to a gate in a fence and continue on the track beyond, over a low col. On the far side of the watershed drop down the left-hand side of a broad valley, cross the West Water and climb to the post on the ridge leading up to the low summit of Cairn Knowe (see map for *Walk 39*).

BARTHOLOMEW WALKS SERIES

Designed to meet the requirements of both experienced and inexperienced walkers, the guides in this series are ideal for anyone who enjoys exploring on foot. They describe the best routes across our greatest walking country from Inverness to the New Forest and Cork & Kerry.

● In each guide, there are at least 30 carefully chosen, easy-to-follow walks over rights of way, with detailed route descriptions accompanying special maps.

● Country walks are graded according to distance and terrain and start from a convenient parking area. The route always returns to the car park, usually by a circular walk and, where appropriate, access by public transport is also possible.

● Notes on local history, geography and wildlife add interest to the walks and the unique notebook format is especially easy to use.

WALK CORK & KERRY
0 7028 0949 7 £4·95

WALK THE CORNISH COASTAL PATH
A special format step-by-step guide to the entire length of the Cornish Coastal Path (Marsland Mouth - Cremyll).
0 7028 0902 0 £4·99

WALK THE COTSWOLDS
0 7028 0908 X £4·99

WALK THE DALES
0 7028 0800 8 £4·99

MORE WALKS IN THE DALES
0 7028 0948 9 £4·95

YORKSHIRE DALES VISITOR'S PACK
Containing a copy of *Walk the Dales* and a folded 1 inch map of the Yorkshire Dales in a clear, plastic carrying wallet.
0 7028 0932 2 £6·99

WALK DARTMOOR
0 7028 0688 9 £3·95

WALK DEVON & CORNWALL
0 7028 1283 8 £4·99

WALK DORSET & HARDY'S WESSEX
0 7028 0906 3 £3·95

WALK EDINBURGH & THE PENTLANDS
0 7028 1280 3 £4·99

WALK EXMOOR & THE QUANTOCKS
0 7028 0910 1 £3·95

WALK HERTS & BUCKS
0 7028 0953 5 £4·95

WALK THE ISLE OF WIGHT
0 7028 1279 X £4·99

WALK THE LAKES
0 7028 8111 2 £4·99

MORE WALKS IN THE LAKES
0 7028 0819 9 £4·99

LAKE DISTRICT WALKING PACK
Containing a copy of *Walk the Lakes* and a folded 1 inch map of the Lake District in a clear, plastic carrying wallet.
0 7028 0876 8 £6·99

WALK LOCH LOMOND & THE TROSSACHS
0 7028 0744 3 £4·99

BARTHOLOMEW WALKS SERIES (Contd)

WALK OBAN, MULL & LOCHABER
0 7028 0801 6 £3·95

WALK THE PEAK DISTRICT
0 7028 0710 9 £4·99

MORE WALKS IN THE PEAK DISTRICT
0 7028 0951 9 £4·95

WALK PERTHSHIRE
0 7028 0766 4 £3·95

WALK LOCH NESS & THE RIVER SPEY
0 7028 0787 7 £3·95

WALK LOTHIAN, THE BORDERS & FIFE
0 7028 0803 2 £3·95

WALK THE NEW FOREST
0 7028 0810 5 £4·99

WALK THE NORTH DOWNS
0 7028 0742 7 £4·99

WALK THE NORTH YORK MOORS
0 7028 0743 5 £4·99

WALK NORTHUMBRIA
0 7028 0959 4 £4·95

NORTHUMBRIA WALKING PACK
Containing a copy of *Walk Northumbria* and a folded copy of the Northumberland & Durham Leisure Map in a clear, plastic carrying wallet.
0 7028 1216 1 £6·99

WALK ROYAL DEESIDE & NORTH EAST SCOTLAND
0 7028 0898 9 £3·95

WALK SNOWDONIA & NORTH WALES
0 7028 0804 0 £3·95

WALK THE SOUTH DOWNS
0 7028 0811 3 £4·99

WALK THE SOUTH PENNINES
0 7028 0955 1 £4·95

WALK SOUTH WALES & THE WYE VALLEY
0 7028 0904 7 £3·95

WALK SOUTH WEST SCOTLAND
0 7028 0900 4 £3·95

Guides in this series may be purchased from good bookshops. In the event of difficulty copies may be obtained by post.
Please send your order with your remittance to
**BARTHOLOMEW BOOKSERVICE BY POST,
PO BOX 29, DOUGLAS, ISLE OF MAN, BRITISH ISLES.**

NAME _____

ADDRESS _____

_____

Please enclose a cheque or postal order made out to 'Bartholomew' for the amount due and allow 25 pence per book postage & packing fee up to a maximum of £3.00.
While every effort is made to keep prices low, it is sometimes necessary to increase cover prices at short notice. Bartholomew reserves the right to show new retail prices on covers which may differ from those previously advertised in the text or elsewhere.